Gardens To Visit

2004

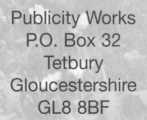

Publicity Works
P.O. Box 32
Tetbury
Gloucestershire
GL8 8BF

Best Wishes.
Tony Russell

Cover picture: Abbey House Gardens (page 107)

Gardens To Visit 2004

Welcome to the second edition of **'Gardens To Visit'** and thank you to the thousands of you who used the first edition to plan your garden visits in 2003.

'Gardens To Visit' is specially created to provide you with all the up to-date information you need to plan your garden visits for the forthcoming year.

Within this edition you will find more than one hundred and twenty of the finest gardens open to the public in the UK. Each garden has its own page which includes a colour photograph, a 140 word description detailing the main features and highlights of the garden and a fact file which provides everything you need to know to plan your visit. It includes location and travelling directions, opening times, admission rates, on-site facilities, advice on how long you need to allow for the visit, a contact person at the garden, website details and much more.

As you browse through **'Gardens To Visit'** you will see there are gardens to visit during every month of the year extending from the north of Scotland right down to the Channel Islands. No matter where you live this book includes gardens worth visiting in your locality.

UK gardens are some of the finest in the world. The unique combination of climate and topography enjoyed by these islands means that plants from right across temperate regions of the world thrive here. Visiting gardens is now given as one of the main reasons for overseas visitors coming to the UK. **'Gardens To Visit'** enables us all to enjoy the diversity, heritage and sheer beauty of the gardens around us.

I hope you enjoy this edition of **'Gardens To Visit'** and may I wish you a very successful and enjoyable season of garden outings in 2004.

Tony Russell

Opposite: Abbotsbury Sub Tropical Gardens (page 31)

Gardens To Visit 2004

Foreword by Tony Russell

£7.99 plus £1.95 P & P

'Gardens To Visit 2004' provides everything you need to know when planning a garden visit.

More than 120 of Britain's finest gardens depicted in all their glory.

The perfect gift for family and friends and the ideal companion for all your garden visits.

To order your copy of 'Gardens To Visit 2004' contact:

WoodLand & Garden Publishing Company
Holmleigh Farm
Huntsgate
Gedney Broadgate
Spalding
Lincs PE12 0DJ

Telephone: 01406 366503
Fax: 01406 366502
Email: derekharris.associates@virgin.net

Publicity Works
P.O. Box 32
Tetbury
Gloucestershire
GL8 8BF

Telephone: 01453 836730
Fax: 01453 835285
Email:mail@publicity-works.org

Contents

Owlpen Manor (page 46)

England

"We met at a tea-table, the silver kettle and the conversation reflecting rhododendrons".

Sir Edwin Lutyens

So what is an English garden? Well, as you explore these pages you will begin to see that such is the diversity and individuality of English gardens, that to capture in one sentence the typical English garden is virtually impossible. It is like attempting to capture in a bottle, the sweet mixed fragrance of Philadelphus and rose after the rain has ceased on a warm June evening.

Be it the garden or the fragrance, enjoy them as you can and commit their charm to memory.

Opposite: Bowood House and Garden / Rhododendron Walks (page 108)

The Swiss Garden was created in the early nineteenth century. It contains picturesque features hidden in an undulating nine-acre landscape. The garden is planted with magnificent trees and ornamental shrubs which are arranged in a series of glades, lawns and winding walks, designed to provide unexpected vistas. The recently refurbished and replanted, subterranean grotto and fernery nestles in the centre. 'The Grand Tour' provided inspiration for the tiny, thatched Swiss Cottage. The fashion for 'Swiss' architecture, so popular in the Regency period can be seen all around the Garden. Elegant floral arches and a network of ponds with decorative bridges and delightful islands complete the picture. Peafowl roam freely in the garden. Spring bulbs, rhododendrons and rambling roses are spectacular in season. Benches are located at frequent intervals. There is also an adjacent picnic area and a woodland lakeside walk.

Fact File

Opening Times:	March - September: Sundays, Bank Holidays 10am - 5pm, all other days 1pm - 5pm. January, February, October: Sundays 10am - 4pm.
Admission Rates:	Adults £3.00, Senior Citizen £2.00, Child Free
Groups Rates:	Minimum group size: 20 but all groups welcome Adults £2.50, Senior Citizen £1.50, Child Free
Facilities:	Restaurant adjacent, Plant Sales.
Disabled Access:	Yes. Toilet and parking for disabled on site. Wheelchairs on loan, booking advised.
Tours/Events:	Tours can be tailored to suit the interests of your group. Popular subjects include the plants and trees, the design and history and the families reponsible for creating this unique garden.
Coach Parking:	Yes
Length of Visit:	2 hours
Booking Contact:	Dulcie Mitchell The Swiss Garden, Old Warden Park, Old Warden, Biggleswade, Bedfordshire, SG18 9ER Telephone: 01767 626244 Fax: 01767 626267
Email:	dmitchell@shuttleworth.org
Website:	www.bedfordshire.gov.uk/swissgarden
Location:	Approximately 2 miles west of Biggleswade A1 roundabout signposted from A1 and A600.

Please quote this guide when booking

From the nine acre garden at Englefield you can look south over the deer park and lake to the Kennet valley and the wooded ridge beyond.

The woodland and water garden, designed and planted by Wallace and Barr in the 1930's, has a magnificent canopy of ancient forest trees underplanted with a wide variety of shrubs and trees including acer, cornus, camellia, magnolia, azalea, davidia and rhododendron. A grotto has lately been built at the top of the stream, lined with a mosaic of varieties of pine cone.

The grey stone balustrades and wide staircases, built in 1860, enclose the lower terraces with their formal planting of mixed borders, roses, topiary, wide lawns and water features. There are small enclosed areas, some lately paved and pebbled, and a children's garden with hidden jets of water from four small statues.

Fact File

Opening Times: Mondays all year. Monday - Thursday inclusive: 1st April - 1st November.
Groups by appointment anytime (minimum 20 people).

Admission Rates: Adults £3.00, Child Free

Facilities: Plant Sales at Englefield Garden Centre (100yrds), Refreshments at Englefield Post Office Stores (150yrds).

Disabled Access: Yes. Parking for disabled on site. Wheelchair on loan, booking necessary.

Tours/Events: None

Coach Parking: Yes

Length of Visit: 1 hour minimum

Booking Contact: Mrs Sleep
Englefield House, Englefield, Reading, Berkshire, RG7 5EN
Telephone: 01189 302221   Fax: 01189 303226

Email: benyon@englefield.co.uk

Website: www.englefield.co.uk

Location: 6 miles west of Reading. 12 miles east of Newbury.
1 1/2 miles from exit 12 of M4 at Theale.
Entrance gate on A340 road to Pangbourne (3 miles).

Waltham Place Organic Farm & Gardens   Berkshire

A magnificent setting, steeped in history, with 40 acres of ornamental gardens integrated into the 170 acre farm. Dutch garden designer, Henk Gerritsen, (of the Priona Gardens), has brought about some exciting changes by combining native and cultivated plants in naturalistic beds within the existing structures of hedges and 17th century walls, continually seeking to explore the boundaries between gardens and nature.

There are a variety of garden areas including the potager, Japanese Garden, butterfly garden, lake and woodlands, parkland meadows and kitchen garden. Complementing these are the newly opened organic farm shop and tearoom.

Fact File

Opening Times: Monday - Friday 10am - 4pm (closed Bank Holidays). 19th April - 30th September.
Admission Rates: Adults £3.50, Senior Citizen £3.50, Child £1.00
Facilities: Organic Farm Shop, Tea Room, Plant Sales, Education Centre.
Disabled Access: Yes. Toilet and parking for disabled on site.
Tours/Events: Monthly seasonal walks, special open days - see website for details.
Coach Parking: Not on site but very close by.
Length of Visit: 2 hours
Booking Contact: Estate Office
Waltham Place, Church Hill, White Waltham, Berks, SL6 3JH
Telephone: 01628 825517 Fax: 01628 825045
Email: estateoffice@walthamplace.com
Website: www.walthamplace.com
Location: From M4 junction 8/9 take A404M and follow signs to White Waltham.
Turn left to Windsor and Paley Street. Farm on left handside.

Please quote this guide when booking

Set in the heart of the Cheshire countryside, Adlington Hall has been the home of the Legh family since 1315. The Hall itself, a magnificent English country house, incorporates Tudor, Elizabethan and Georgian architecture and houses a 17th century organ played by Handel.

The 2,000 acre Estate, landscaped in the 18th century, contains beautiful gardens in the style of 'Capability' Brown complete with a ha-ha. The ancient Lime Avenue, dating from 1688, leads to a woodland 'Wilderness' with winding paths, temples, bridges and follies. A path through the Laburnum Arcade leads into the formal Rose Garden, then on to the Maze created in English Yew. The Father Tiber Water Garden provides a peaceful haven with its ponds, fountains and water cascade and the newly created Penstemon Garden provides a colourful addition to the East Wing. Other features include a large herbaceous border, rockeries, specimen trees, azaleas and rhododendrons.

Fact File

Opening Times: June, July, August: Wednesday only 2pm - 5pm.
Open weekdays throughout the year for groups by prior arrangement.

Admission Rates: Adults £5.00, Senior Citizen £5.00, Child £2.00

Groups Rates: Minimum group size: 20
Adults £4.00, Senior Citizen £4.00, Child £2.00

Facilities: Tea Room.

Disabled Access: Limited. Toilet and parking for disabled on site.

Tours/Events: Guided tours by appointment. Please telephone for details of special events.

Coach Parking: Yes

Length of Visit: 3 hours

Booking Contact: The Guide
Adlington Hall, Adlington, Macclesfield, Cheshire, SK10 4LF
Telephone: 01625 820875   Fax: 01625 828756

Email: enquiries@adlingtonhall.com

Website: www.adlingtonhall.com

Location: 5 miles north of Macclesfield off A523 turn left at Adlington crossroads onto Mill Lane. Entrance 1/2 mile on left.

Please quote this guide when booking

These award winning Grade II listed gardens were recently voted one of the top 50 gardens in Europe. Lovingly created by successive generations of the family, and still in private ownership, the gardens at Arley reflect a by-gone age. Paths lead you in and out of smaller gardens, each with a different theme and atmosphere, from the shaded Herb Garden to the Flag Garden and on to the "oldest and finest double herbaceous borders in the country". Explore the unique Ilex columns, wander down through the Sundial Garden to the Victorian Rootree. The family Hall is open to the public on Tuesdays and Sundays. With a family Chapel, gift shop, plant nursery and Tudor Barn Restaurant, Arley offers a peaceful day out.

Events include outdoor concerts, antique fairs, plant fairs, The ARLEY GARDEN FESTIVAL, 26 - 27 June, A Christmas Floral Extravaganza and new for 2004, THE ARLEY COUNTRY FAIR, 31 July - 1 August.

Fact File

Opening Times: Tuesday - Sunday & Bank Holidays 11am - 5pm.
Easter - 26th September & October weekends.

Admission Rates: Adults £4.50, Senior Citizen £3.90, Child £2.00, (Gardens only, Hall extra)

Groups Rates: Adults £3.85, Senior Citizen £3.35, Child £2.00. (Gardens only)

Facilities: Shop, Teas, Restaurant, Plant Sales, Picnic Areas, Free Parking, Walks on the Estate.

Disabled Access: Yes. Toilet and parking for disabled on site. Wheelchairs on loan, booking necessary.

Tours/Events: Special tours by Head Gardener & Lord & Lady Ashbrook may be booked at extra charge.
Hall tours also available at extra cost.

Coach Parking: Yes

Length of Visit: 2 - 3 hours

Booking Contact: Mrs Shelagh Bebington
Arley Hall, Arley, Nr Northwich, Cheshire, CW9 6NA
Telephone: 01565 777353 ext 30 Fax: 01565 777465

Email: enquiries@arleyestate.zuunet.co.uk

Website: www.arleyhallandgardens.com

Location: Brown signs from M6 (junction 19 or 20), M56 (junction 9 or 10),
A556 Knutsford and A49 Northwich.

Please quote this guide when booking

Cholmondeley Castle Garden is said by many to be among the most romantically beautiful gardens they have seen. Even the wild orchids, daisies and buttercups take on an aura of glamour in this beautifully landscaped setting. Visitors enter by the deer park mere - one of two strips of water which are home to many types of waterfowl and freshwater fish. Those who take advantage of the picnic site can walk round the lake and enjoy the splendid view of the Gothic Castle which stands so dramatically on the hill surrounded by sweeping lawns and magnificent trees; two enormous cedars of lebanon and great spreading oaks among sweet chestnut, lime, beech and plane. Whatever the season there is always a wealth of plants and shrubs in flower from the earliest bulbs through many varieties of magnolia, camellia, azalea and rhododendrons, followed by a golden canopied laburnum grove, a very fine davidia involucrata in the glade, and varieties of cornus. There is also a very pretty rose garden surrounded by mixed borders, containing a large variety of herbaceous plants and shrubs.

Fact File

Opening Times:	Sunday 4th April - Sunday 26th September.
	Wednesday, Thursday, Sunday (Bank Holiday Mondays and Good Friday).
Admission Rates:	Adults £3.50, Child £1.50
Groups Rates:	Minimum group size: 25
	Please ring to confirm.
Facilities:	Shop, Plant Sales, Teas.
Disabled Access:	Yes. Toilet and parking for disabled on site.
Tours/Events:	Please ring to enquire about special events, plant fares, plays, concerts.
Coach Parking:	Yes
Length of Visit:	3 - 4 hours
Booking Contact:	Cholmondeley Castle, Malpas, Cheshire, SY14 8AH
	Telephone: 01829 720383 Fax: 01829 720877
Email:	pennypritchard@supanet.com
Website:	Currently being developed
Location:	7 miles west of Nantwich, 6 miles north of Whitchurch on A49.

Surrounding the 18th century house Dunham Massey's has been described as one of the North West's great plantsmans's gardens. The varied site and acid conditions provide for a wide range of unusual shade and moisture loving plants including Giant Chinese Lilies, Himalayan Blue Poppies and rare late flowering azaleas, all set amongst lawns, mixed borders and waterside plantings.

Magnificent trees are reflected in the Elizabethan moat, the richly planted borders are vibrant with colour all through the year and historical features like the Orangery, Mount and Well House complement the sweeping lawns. A garden of contrasts, the shady woodland has drifts of bluebells in spring, the Edwardian Parterre a glorious summer show of formal bedding and the hydrangea border comes into its own as the days shorten into Autumn. A garden to go back to again and again.

Fact File

Opening Times: House & Garden open Sat 27 March, close 2 Nov. House open Sat to Wed, Garden daily. NOTE: House also open Good Friday. House open 12 - 5pm (11 - 5pm Bank Holiday Sun, Mon & Good Friday). Garden open 11 - 5.30pm. House & garden close an hour earlier from 24 Oct. Park, Restaurant & Shop open daily all year (except Restaurant closed Christmas Day, Shop closed Christmas Day & Boxing Day).

Admission Rates: **National Trust Members Free.** Parking £3.50. House & Garden Adults £6.00, Child £3.00, Family £15.00. House or Garden: £4.00/£2.00. **Groups Rates:** Min group size: 15 - £5.00.

Facilities: Visitor Centre, Shop, Plant Sales, Teas, Restaurant.

Disabled Access: Yes. Toilet and parking for disabled on site. Wheelchairs on loan, booking necessary.

Tours/Events: Guided Garden Tours most Mondays & Wednesdays at 11.30 & 2.30. Special Events through year, please call for details.

Coach Parking: Yes. **Length of Visit:** 3 plus hours.

Booking Contact: Visitor Services. The National Trust, Dunham Massey Hall, Altrincham, WA14 4SJ Telephone: 0161 941 1025 Fax: 0161 929 7508

Email: dunhammassey@nationaltrust.org.uk

Website: www.nationaltrust.org.uk

Location: Altrincham, Cheshire.

Photography by Mrs V Anderson

Approximate 100 acres of Woodland Gardens and natural woodland bordering the Lynher Estuary featuring extensive woodlands and riverside walks.

The garden contains a national collection of *Camellia japonica*. There are a wide variety of camellias, magnolias, rhododendrons and other flowering trees and shrubs, numerous wild flowers and birds in beautiful surrounds.

Fact File

Opening Times:	11am to 5.30pm, everyday excluding Mondays and Fridays. Open Bank Holiday Monday. 1st March to 31st October.
Admission Rates:	Adults £3.50, Senior Citizen £3.50, Child under 16 free
Groups Rates:	As admission rates.
Facilities:	Teas, Restaurant, Shop (Available only on Antony House open days).
Disabled Access:	Yes over rough terrain in parts. Parking for disabled on site.
Tours/Events:	Tours available for parties on request.
Coach Parking:	Yes
Length of Visit:	Between 1 and 2 hours
Booking Contact:	Mrs V Anderson Antony, Torpoint, Cornwall, PL11 2QA Telephone: 01752 812364
Email:	paul.cressy@colvilles.co.uk
Website:	None
Location:	From the A38 Trerulefoot roundabout follow brown tourist signs for Antony House. At Antony House continue past the house down the drive. The Woodland Gardens can be found on the left hand side.

Please quote this guide when booking

One of only three Grade I listed Cornish Gardens set within the 865 acres of the Country Park overlooking the Plymouth Sound. Sir Richard Edgcumbe of Cotehele built a new home in his deer park at Mount Edgcumbe in 1547. Miraculously the walls of his red stone Tudor House survived a direct hit by bombs in 1941 and it was restored by the 6th Earl in 1958. It is now beautifully furnished with family possessions. The two acre Earl's Garden was created beside the House in the 18th century. Ancient and rare trees including a 400 year old lime, a splendid Lucombe oak and a Mexican pine, are set amidst classical garden houses and an exotic Shell Seat. Colourful flowers and heather grace the re-created Victorian East Lawn terrace. Also Formal 18th century Gardens in Italian, French & English style, modern American & New Zealand sections. There are over 1000 varieties in the National Camellia Collection which received the international award of 'Camellia Garden of Excellence'.

Fact File

Opening Times: House & Earls Garden open 4th April - 30th September, Sunday to Thursday 11am - 4.30pm. Country Park open all year.

Admission Rates: Adults £4.50, Senior Citizen £3.50, Child £2.25

Groups Rates: Minimum group size: 10 (March - October)
Adults £3.50, Senior Citizen £3.50, Child £2.00

Facilities: Shop & Tea Room in House.
Orangery Restaurant (limited opening in winter), Civil Weddings, Conference Facilities.

Disabled Access: Yes. Toilet and parking for disabled on site. Wheelchairs on loan, booking necessary.

Tours/Events: Guided tours of the gardens available all year. Historic Buildings, Camellia Collection in season. Exhibitions and events programme.

Coach Parking: Yes

Length of Visit: 2 hours

Booking Contact: Secretary. Mount Edgcumbe House, Cremyll, Torpoint, Cornwall, PL10 1HZ
Telephone: 01752 822236 Fax: 01752 822199

Email: mt.edgcumbe@plymouth.gov.uk **Website:** www.cornwalltouristboard.co.uk

Location: From Plymouth Cremyll Foot Ferry, Torpoint Ferry or Saltash Bridge.
From Cornwall via Liskeard - to A374, B3247, follow brown signs.

Please quote this guide when booking

Pencarrow, a Georgian house with 50 acres of Grade 2 star listed Gardens, must be one of Cornwall's finest stately homes. It is still privately owned and lived in by the Molesworth-St Aubyn's, who purchased the estate in the reign of Queen Elizabeth I. Pencarrow lies at the foot of a valley midway between Bodmin and Wadebridge. It is approached through a mile long drive flanked by well planned woodland, nearly 700 varieties of rhododendrons, camellias and hydrangeas. The imposing Palladian style house built in 1771, contains a superb collection of paintings by many famous artists, including a unique collection of works by Sir Joshua Reynolds, set amongst outstanding furniture and porcelain. In 1882 during his visit Sir Arthur Sullivan composed much of the music for his comic opera "Iolanthe". Pencarrow was the National Heritage Award winner in 1997, 98 and 99 (also voted by its its visitors "Best Historic House in the United Kingdom").

Fact File

Opening Times: The House & Gardens open Sundays to Thursdays, 28th March to 28th October, 11am - 4pm (last tour). Tea Room and Craft Gallery are open from 11am to 5pm Sundays to Thursdays.

Groups Rates: Minimum group size: 20 - 30, **(£1 off the normal entry price), ie House & Garden** Adults £6.00, Child £3.00, Gardens only Adults £3.00, Child Free. Group 30 plus, House & Garden £5.00, Gardens only £2.50. House tours are conducted in a maximum group of 20 persons and take approx one hour. Groups above this number are split into 2 groups.

Facilities: House, Shop, Craft Gallery, Plant Sales, Children's Play Area, Tea Rooms, Licensed Restaurant.

Disabled Access: Yes. Toilet and parking for disabled on site. Wheelchairs on loan, booking necessary.

Tours/Events: Guided tours around the house (last tour 4pm) - Garden tours for group bookings. Jazz in Gardens, Theatre, Concerts, Fun Evenings, Conference Room, Wedding License.

Coach Parking: Yes **Length of Visit:** 2 1/2 - 5 hours

Booking Contact: James Reynolds. Pencarrow, Washaway, Bodmin, Cornwall, PL30 3AG Telephone: 01208 841369 Fax: 01208 841722

Email: pencarrow@aol.com **Website:** www.pencarrow.co.uk

Location: Four miles north west of Bodmin, signed off the A389 and B3266 at Washaway.

Please quote this guide when booking

The 30-acre estate comprises gardens within a garden which hold a wide range of some 6000 plants, all of which are labelled. In addition to rhododendrons, magnolias and camellias so familiar in Cornish gardens here are Mediterranean and southern-hemisphere plants grown for all year round interest. Herbaceous borders, a fernery, a formal garden, a woodland walk, shrubberies and a wild flower meadow. The water features include a large wildlife pond, an ornamental pond with cascades (stocked with koi carp), a lake with an island (home for black swans and water fowl) and marsh gardens. Trees are also a speciality with an acer glade, a collection of 80 conifers, all different, in a four acre Pinetum, an Arboretum and an acre Japanese garden. Holder of the National collection of Grevilleas. Seeds brought back on Seed Hunting Expeditions every year for our Nursery of Rare & Unusual Plants. The gardens were given a Highly Commended Award by the Cornish Tourist Board for 2002.

Fact File

Opening Times: March - End of October.
Nursery all year.
Admission Rates: Adults £4.50, Senior Citizen £4.50, Child £2.50
Groups Rates: Minimum group size: 20
Facilities: Plant Sales, Tea Room, Shop.
Disabled Access: Partial. Toilet and parking for disabled on site. Wheelchairs on loan, booking necessary.
Tours/Events: Tours everyday, booking essential. Wood Turning demonstration everyday.
Coach Parking: Yes
Length of Visit: 3 hours
Booking Contact: Shirley Clemo
Pine Lodge Gardens, Holmbush, St Austell, Cornwall, PL25 3RQ
Telephone: 01726 73500   Fax: 01726 77370
Email: garden@pine-lodge.co.uk
Website: www.pine-lodge.co.uk
Location: Situated on the A390 2 miles east of St Austell.

Please quote this guide when booking

Steeply wooded 25 acre sub-tropical ravine garden falls 200 feet from 18th century house to private beach on Helford River.

A stream cascades over waterfalls through ponds full of Koi Carp and exotic water plants, winds through 2 acres of blue and white hydrangeas and spills out over the beach. Huge Australian tree ferns and palms mingle with shrubs of ever changing colours and scent beneath over-arching canopy of 100 year old rhododendrons and magnolias. A giant plantation of gunnera and clumps of huge bamboos give the garden a unique and exotic wildness matched by no other garden in the British Isles.

The newly built Hibbert Centre houses a distinctive restaurant, garden and gift shop and a gallery where fine art is for sale.

Fact File

Opening Times:	Open every day of the year 10.30am to 5pm.
Admission Rates:	Adults £5.00, Senior Citizen £4.50, Child £3.00
Groups Rates:	Minimum group size: 12
	Adults £4.00, Senior Citizen £4.00, Child £2.00
Facilities:	Visitor Centre, Shop, Plant Sales, Teas, Restaurant, Selling Art Gallery in the Hibbert Centre.
Disabled Access:	Yes. Toilet and parking for disabled on site. Wheelchairs on loan, booking necessary.
Tours/Events:	Free welcome talk on arrival, full guided tour of one and a half hours at an extra £1 per head - must be booked in advance.
Coach Parking:	Yes
Length of Visit:	2 1/2 - 3 hours
Booking Contact:	V Woodcroft
	Trebah Garden, Mawnan Smith, Falmouth, Cornwall, TR11 5JZ
	Telephone: 01326 250448 Fax: 01326 250781
Email:	mail@trebah-garden.co.uk
Website:	www.trebah-garden.co.uk
Location:	From north - A39 from Truro to Treliever Cross Roundabout, follow brown and white tourism signs to Trebah.

Please quote this guide when booking

Trevarno Estate Gardens & National Museum of Gardening   Cornwall

A unique and unforgettable gardening experience comprising sixty acres of beautiful Victorian and Georgian Gardens and Ground, the amazing National Museum of Gardening and a range of fascinating craft workshops and display areas inspired by the estate and gardens. Trevarno is a jewel in the Cornish crown having one of the counties largest and most diverse plant collections, many contrasting features, abundant wildlife and a major restoration project within two walled gardens. After exploring the tranquil woodland walks, lakeside terraces, mysterious rockery and grotto, and more formal areas including the Sunken Italian Garden and Serpentine Yew Tunnel, relax and enjoy homemade refreshments amongst the sub-tropical plants in the delightful Fountain Garden Conservatory. But leave plenty of time to see the unique National Museum of Gardening, a fascinating celebration of Britain's glorious gardening heritage. Don't forget the famous Handmade Soap Workshop and New Museum, Britain's first accredited Organic Herbal Workshop.

Fact File

Opening Times: 10.30am - 5pm all year.

Admission Rates: Adults £4.75, Senior Citizen £4.20, Child £1.75, Disabled £2.50

Groups Rates: Minimum group size: 12
Adults £4.25, Senior Citizen £3.75, Child £1.25

Facilities: The National Museum of Gardening, Shop, Plant Sales, Teas, Craft Workshops, Soap Collection, *Vintage Toy Collection (*small additional charge).

Disabled Access: Partial. Toilet and parking for disabled on site. Wheelchairs on loan, booking essential.

Tours/Events: Numerous Charity events throughout the year. Please call for details.

Coach Parking: Yes, for up to 6 coaches.

Length of Visit: 4 hours

Booking Contact: Garden Co-ordinator
Trevarno Estate, Trevarno Manor, Crowntown, Nr Helston, Cornwall, TR13 0RU
Telephone: 01326 574274   Fax: 01326 574282

Email: info@trevarnoestate.fsnet.co.uk

Website: Under construction.

Location: Trevarno is located immediately east of Crowntown village - leave Helston on Penzance Road and follow the brown signs.

Please quote this guide when booking

Trewithen means 'house of the trees' and the name truly describes this fine early Georgian house in its splendid setting of wood and parkland.

Country Life described the house as 'one of the outstanding West Country houses of the 18th century' and Penelope Hobhouse has described the garden as 'perhaps the most beautiful woodland garden in England'.

2004 is the 100th year in which George Johnstone inherited Trewithen and started developing the gardens as we know them today. The great glade on the south side is a masterpiece of landscape gardening and is a monument to the genius of George Johnstone. These gardens covering some thirty acres are renowned for their magnificent collection of camellias, rhododendrons, magnolias and many rare trees and shrubs which are seldom found elsewhere in Britain. The extensive woodland gardens are surrounded by traditional landscaped parkland.

Fact File

Opening Times:	Open 1st March to 30th September, 10am to 4.30pm Monday to Saturday. Sundays (April and May only).
Admission Rates:	Adults £4.25
Groups Rates:	Minimum group size: 20 Group £4.00 per person
Facilities:	Trewithen Tea Shop, Plant Sales, Camera Obscura, Viewing Platforms.
Disabled Access:	Yes. Toilet and parking for disabled on site. Wheelchairs on loan.
Tours/Events:	Guided tours available, prior booking is essential. Occasional special events please telephone for details.
Coach Parking:	Yes
Length of Visit:	2 - 2 1/2 hours
Booking Contact:	Glenys Cates Trewithen Gardens, Grampound Road, Nr Truro, Cornwall, TR2 4DD Telephone: 01726 883647 Fax: 01726 882301
Email:	gardens@trewithen-estate.demon.co.uk
Website:	www.trewithengardens.co.uk
Location:	On the A390 between Truro and St Austell.

Please quote this guide when booking

Something old, something new. The garden has some twelve rockeries discovered as the undergrowth was cleared from the surrounding woodland. Built when the house (a vicarage) was rebuilt in the 1830s, the largest is some 25-30 feet high and planted with colourful shrubs and plants. Beside it is a small lake planted along the margins with primulas, lilies and herbaceous plants. The Dell Garden, a smaller double rockery, is alive early in the year with spring bulbs and plants.

Immediately around the house are the original Italian terraces and, since 1994, the landscaped lawns have been embellished with extensive herbaceous beds, a 150-foot-long rose pergola intersecting a magnolia walk, a hydrangea walk backed with cherry trees and a canal leading to a small pond, all showing how sympathetically new ideas can blend with old. Brenda propagates and sells many plants from the garden.

Fact File

Opening Times: Sundays and Tuesdays 2pm - 5.30pm. Groups by arrangement including other days.
Admission Rates: Adults £3.00, Senior Citizen £3.00, Child (6 - 16yrs) 50p, under 5 Free
Groups Rates: Minimum group size: 6
Adults £2.50
Facilities: Plant Sales, Cream Teas.
Disabled Access: Majority of garden accessible. Parking for disabled on site.
Tours/Events: Guided tours of garden by arrangement.
Coach Parking: No but available along the road (or in village). Please telephone for information.
Length of Visit: 1 1/2 hours
Booking Contact: G W Salmon
Trist House, Veryan, Truro, Cornwall, TR2 5QA
Telephone: 01872 501422 Fax: 01872 501211
Email: graham@tristobs.ndo.uk
Website: None
Location: Veryan is just off the A3078 from Tregony to St Mawes. Trist House is the first drive on the right past the Post Office stores.

Please quote this guide when booking

Brantwood's gardens and estate are like no other. Mature Victorian landscape gardens lead to Ruskin's own experimental landscapes, to ancient woodlands, high Moorland and spectacular views. Completion of the Zig-Zaggy, a garden begun by John Ruskin 130 years ago, and the High Walk, a spectacular Victorian viewing platform, brings a total of eight gardens restored at Brantwood. Expect the unexpected and explore 250 acres of fascinating landscape.

Whichever season you choose to visit you are assured year round interest. Spectacular azaleas in springtime; a collection of ferns, herbs and colourful herbaceous borders in summer; the vibrant colours of autumn; or a winter snowfall can transform the gardens into a winter wonderland.

Stroll the paths, sit and marvel at the magnificent views. Whatever you chose to do, you will take home with you the discovery of John Ruskin's legacy and inspiration.

Fact File

Opening Times:	Mid - March to mid - November daily 11am - 5.30pm.
	Mid - November to mid - March Wednesday - Sunday 11am - 4.30pm.
Admission Rates:	Adults £5.50 / £3.75 garden only, Child £1.00
Groups Rates:	Minimum group size: 10
	Adults £4.50 / £3.00 garden only, Child £.1.00
Facilities:	Shop, Plant Sales, Restaurant, Craft Gallery.
Disabled Access:	Partial. Toilet and parking for disabled on site. Wheelchair on loan, booking necessary.
Tours/Events:	A wide variety of events await, please check website for details.
Coach Parking:	Yes but limited.
Length of Visit:	4 - 6 hours
Booking Contact:	Josie Coombe
	Brantwood, Coniston, Cumbria, LA21 8AD
	Telephone: 01539 441396 Fax: 01539 441263
Email:	josie@brantwood.org.uk
Website:	www.brantwood.org.uk
Location:	2 1/4 miles east of Coniston. Signposted from Coniston.

Please quote this guide when booking

Holker Hall & Gardens   Cumbria

At Holker Hall our aim is to ensure you always feel like a welcome guest not a tourist. Our visitors wander freely throughout this 'best-loved' of stately homes never impeded by ropes or barriers.

The 25 acres of gardens the pride of Lord and Lady Cavendish offer rare treats and allow for personal discoveries. The newly created labyrinth in the wildflower meadow offers an opportunity for quiet contemplation. Stroll through our other 200 acres of grounds and perhaps enjoy a picnic while you see fallow deer frolic.

Treat yourself to a wonderful Cumbrian lunch in the Courtyard Café. Plants from our nursery, unique gifts and specialty products all hand selected by Lady Cavendish are available in our Gift Shop. To complete your day make time to visit the Lakeland Motor Museum, featuring the Campbell Bluebird Legend Exhibition and an extensive collection of transport and motoring memorabilia.

Fact File

Opening Times:	28th March - 31st October. Open Sunday to Friday (closed Saturday).
	Gates open 10am, last admission 4.30pm.
Admission Rates:	Hall, Gardens & Motor Museum, Adults £8.75, Senior Citizen £8.75, Child £5.00
Groups Rates:	Minimum group size: 20
	Adults £6.75, Senior Citizen £5.75, Child £4.00 (Please telephone to confirm).
Facilities:	Visitor Centre, Shop, Plant Sales, Teas, Restaurant and new for 2004 The Holker Food Hall.
Disabled Access:	Yes. Toilet and parking for disabled on site. Wheelchairs on loan, booking necessary.
Tours/Events:	Guided tour of Hall, Gardens or to Ice House available to groups.
	Holker Garden Festival 4th - 6th June.
Coach Parking:	Yes
Length of Visit:	2 - 4 hours
Booking Contact:	Elizabeth Moss
	Holker Hall, Cark-in-Cartmel, Nr Grange-over-Sands, Cumbria, LA11 7PR
	Telephone: 015395 58328 Fax: 015395 58378
Email:	publicopening@holker.co.uk
Website:	www.holker-hall.co.uk
Location:	New M6 junction 36, follow Brown & White Tourist signs through Grange-over-Sands.

Please quote this guide when booking

Set in the dramatic grandeur of the Lakeland Fells, the wild, woodland gardens are home to an incredible collection of rare and beautiful plants. Miles of paths wind through this extra-ordinary scenery, which also provides cover for a varied wildlife population. A great plant-hunting tradition flourishes at Muncaster and many of the plants in the gardens are now highly endangered in their native habitats due to population pressures and deforestation. Thousands of specimens, particularly from China and the Far East, have been grown from seed collected on recent expeditions around the turn of the Third Millennium. British plants too flourish in abundance, and the bluebells in the high woods should not be missed in late April and early May. Gardens evolve and change, and no matter what time of year you visit, there is always something in flower and new discoveries to be made. And the highlight: the view from the Castle and Terrace is truly "Heaven's Gate" as described by John Ruskin, the 19th Century father of the conservation movement.

Fact File

Opening Times:	14th March - 7th November, open daily 10.30am.
Admission Rates:	Please telephone for details.
Groups Rates:	Minimum group size: 12
	Please telephone for details of group rates.
Facilities:	3 Shops, Café, Play Area for children.
Disabled Access:	Yes. Toilet and parking for disabled on site. Electric wheelchair on loan, booking necessary.
Tours/Events:	Fantasia of Rhododendrons April/May, Bluebell Heaven last 2 weeks April,
	RHS Annual Muncaster lecture May.
	Private garden tours can be arranged.
Coach Parking:	Yes
Length of Visit:	3 1/2 hours
Booking Contact:	Joanne Hall
	Muncaster Castle, Ravenglass, Cumbria, CA18 1RQ
	Telephone: 01229 717614 Fax: 01229 717010
Email:	info@muncaster.co.uk
Website:	www.muncaster.co.uk
Location:	1 mile south of Ravenglass.

Please quote this guide when booking

Spanning nearly 300 years of horticultural history, Bicton Park Botanical Gardens are set in the picturesque Otter Valley, where the gentle climate ensures a magnificent display of exotic plants throughout the year. From the classical grandeur of the 18th century Italian Garden, Bicton's 63 acres (25.5 ha) extend through less formal gardens to a superbly landscaped parkland with lakes, streams, a nature trail and Devon's largest collection of record-holding trees. Twenty-five conifers and broadleaf specimens have been officially recognised as the tallest or largest of their kind in the British Isles. Bicton's 19th century Palm House is one of the world's most beautiful garden buildings. Many other tropical plants and cacti are also displayed under cover, as are the fascinating exhibits in the Countryside Museum and Shell House. For a small extra charge, visitors may tour Bicton Park on Britain's only 18-inch gauge passenger-carrying railway.

Fact File

Opening Times: Daily all year (except Christmas Day) from 10am - 6pm in spring/summer and 10am - 5pm in autumn/winter.

Admission Rates: Adults £4.95, Senior Citizen £3.95, Child £3.95

Groups Rates: Minimum group size: 16
Adults £3.75, Senior Citizen £3.75, Child £3.25

Facilities: Restaurant, gift shop, garden centre, kiosk's, picnic area, children's indoor and outdoor play areas, mini-golf course.

Disabled Access: Yes. Toilet and parking for disabled on site. Wheelchairs on loan by prior arrangement.

Tours/Events: Walks for groups by prior arrangement. Tours may be tailored to your special interests, including history, trees, wildlife.

Coach Parking: Yes   **Length of Visit:** 3 hours minimum all day max

Booking Contact: Heather / Valerie / Simon. Bicton Park Botanical Gardens, East Budleigh, Budleigh Salterton, Devon, EX9 7BJ. Telephone: 01395 568465   Fax: 01395 568374

Email: simon@bictongardens.co.uk   **Website:** www.bictongardens.co.uk

Location: Bicton is 10 miles SE of Exeter. From M5 leave at junction 30 and follow the brown 'Bicton Park' signs. The gardens are midway between Budleigh Salterton and Newton Poppleford on the B3178.

Docton Mill & Gardens   North Devon

Docton Mill is situated in a stunning valley 1000m from the coast. The Garden started in the 1930's but fell into disrepair in the 1970's. 1980 saw the Mill renovated and Garden cleared with extensive planting and the creation of a new Bog Garden and borders, vast numbers of trees were planted. The start of the new Millennium saw developments including a new Magnolia Garden with large Herbaceous borders, Woodland Garden and Greenhouse area enabling more extensive plant propagation.

The Garden theme is to make everything as natural as possible. In spring there are displays of narcissi, primulas, camellias, rhododendrums, azaleas with bluebells covering the woods. In summer the garden abounds with roses, there is a rosebank of Felicia and Pax and adjacent to this is the Herbaceous border. In this field there are 25 varieties of magnolia - truly a garden to give variety throughout the seasons.

Fact File

Opening Times:	10am - 6pm - 1st March to 31st October inclusive.
Admission Rates:	Adults £3.50, Senior Citizen £3.00, Child £1.00
Groups Rates:	Minimum group size: 20
	Adults £3.00, Senior Citizen £3.00, Child £1.00
Facilities:	Tearoom, Plant Sales, Light Lunches available till 5pm.
Disabled Access:	Please ring, as we can explain the level of suitability for people with disabilities.
Tours/Events:	Guided tours of garden can be arranged but would need to be pre-booked.
Coach Parking:	No, parking available off site.
Length of Visit:	2 hours minimum
Booking Contact:	John or Lana Borrett
	Docton Mill, Lymebridge, Hartland, North Devon, EX39 6EA
	Telephone: 01237 441369 Fax: 01237 441369
Email:	john@doctonmill.freeserve.co.uk
Website:	www.doctonmill.co.uk
Location:	From A39 between Bideford & Bude, follow brown tourist 'Flower' signs or refer to our website.

Please quote this guide when booking

Hartland Abbey Gardens North Devon

Hartland Abbey is situated in a beautiful, wooded valley leading to an Atlantic cove. Consecrated in 1160 as an Augustinian monastery, on the Dissolution it was given by Henry VIII to the Sergeant of his Wine Cellar whose descendants live here today. It contains fascinating architecture and collections of paintings, furniture, porcelain, early photographs and documents from 1160.

Intimate paths designed by Gertrude Jekyll wind through woodland gardens of spring bulbs, rhododendrons, azaleas, camellias and hydrangeas. Huge gunnera thrive in The Bog Garden which leads to the Victorian Fernery, lost since 1914, and only discovered recently. Charming 18th century Walled Gardens contain many tender and rare plants, climbers, roses, herbaceous perennials and huge echium pininana. Vegetables, fruit and herbs once again flourish here. Glasshouses provide tender plants for the Abbey. Peacocks, black sheep and donkeys roam in the Parkland.

Fact File

Opening Times: House & Garden: 2pm - 5.30pm, Wednesdays, Thursdays, Sundays & Bank Holidays plus Tuesdays in July & August, 1st April - 3rd October.
Gardens only: 2pm - 5.30pm, 1st April - 3rd October daily except Saturdays.

Admission Rates: House & Garden: Adults £6.00, Senior Citizen £5.50, Child (over 9) £1.50
Garden only: Adults £4.00, Senior Citizen £4.00, Child (over 9) 50p

Groups Rates: Minimum group size: 12 (Groups can visit at other times & dates by prior appointment)
Adults £5.00, Senior Citizen £4.50, Child £1.50

Facilities: Shop, Museum, Cream Teas, Small Plant Sales.

Disabled Access: Partial. Toilet and parking for disabled on site.

Tours/Events: None

Coach Parking: Yes **Length of Visit:** House & Gardens: 2 1/2 - 3 hours, Gardens only: 2 hours

Booking Contact: Mary Heard
Hartland Abbey, Hartland, Nr Bideford, North Devon, EX39 6DT
Telephone: 01237 441264 Fax: 01237 441264

Website: www.hartlandabbey.com

Location: 15 miles west of Bideford, 15 miles north of Bude off A39 between Hartland and Quay. Map will be sent showing easy coach access.

Please quote this guide when booking

Set deep in the lovely North Devon countryside, RHS Garden Rosemoor has now come of age as a garden of national importance. Lady Anne Berry gifted Rosemoor to the RHS 11 years ago, since then the original eight acres have been greatly developed.

To the huge range of plants collected by Lady Anne, the RHS has added features such as the Formal Garden, extensive herbaceous borders, herb and cottage gardens, a potager, the Foliage and Plantsman's Garden and extensive stream and lakeside plantings. Recent additions include the Mediterranean and semi-tropical plantings which have been thriving during the recent long hot summers and the newly planted Winter Garden. But what is perhaps the most popular feature of this delightful garden is the extensive rose garden, proving beyond doubt the lie that the West Country cannot produce beautiful roses.

"Voted South West Visitor Attraction of the Year 2003".

Fact File

Opening Times: April - September 10am - 6pm, October - March 10am - 5pm, open every day except Christmas Day. Visitor Centre open 2nd January - 24th December.

Admission Rates: Adults £5.00, Senior Citizen £5.00, Child £1.00, RHS Members Free

Groups Rates: Minimum group size: 10
Adults £4.50, Senior Citizen £4.50, Child £1.00

Facilities: Visitor Centre, Shop, Restaurant, Kiosk, Plant Sales.

Disabled Access: Yes. Toilet and parking for disabled on site. Wheelchairs on loan, booking necessary.

Tours/Events: Full programme of events throughout the year.

Coach Parking: Yes

Length of Visit: 2 hours

Booking Contact: Helen Foster-Collins
RHS Garden Rosemoor, Great Torrington, North Devon, EX38 8PH
Telephone: 01805 624067   Fax: 01805 624717

Email: helenf@rhs.org.uk

Website: www.rhs.org.uk

Location: 1 mile south of Torrington on the A3124 (formerly B3220).

Please quote this guide when booking

Established in 1765 by the first Countess of Ilchester. Developed since then into a 20-acre grade 1 listed magnificent woodland valley garden. World famous for its Camellia Groves, Magnolias, Rhododendron and Hydrangea collections. In summer it is awash with colour.

Since the restoration after the great storm of 1990 many new and exotic plants have been introduced. The Garden is now a mixture of formal and informal, with a charming walled garden and spectacular woodland valley views.

Facilities include a Colonial Tea House for lunches, snacks and drinks, a Plant Centre and quality Gift Shop. Events such as Shakespeare and concerts are presented during the year. The Floodlighting of the Garden at the end of October should not be missed.

Fact File

Opening Times:	Summer - 10am to 6pm, last entry 5pm.
	Winter (November - February) - 10am to 4pm or dusk, last entry 1 hour before.
Admission Rates:	Adults £6.50, Senior Citizen £6.00, Child £3.75
Groups Rates:	Minimum group size: 10
	Adults £5.50, Senior Citizen £5.00, Child £3.00
Facilities:	Colonial Tea House, Gift Shop, Plant Centre.
Disabled Access:	Yes, 50% of garden accessible. Toilet and parking for disabled on site. Wheelchairs on loan.
Tours/Events:	£1 per person (minimum charge £15) on top of the group rate (minimum 10 people).
	Special events see web site.
Coach Parking:	Yes
Length of Visit:	2 hours
Booking Contact:	Jess Owen. Abbotsbury Sub Tropical Garden, Bullers Way, Abbotsbury, (Nr Weymouth), Dorset, DT3 4LA. Telephone: 01305 871130 Fax: 01305 871092
Email:	info@abbotsbury-tourism.co.uk
Website:	www.abbotsbury-tourism.co.uk
Location:	On the B3157 between Weymouth and Bridport in Dorset. Come off the A35 near Dorchester at Winterborne Abbas.

Please quote this guide when booking

The contemporary parkland and pleasure gardens were laid out in the "Jardin Anglais" style popularised by Capability Brown, which consisted of rolling turf, carefully placed groups of trees and a lake. The lovely 35 acre formal gardens were created between 1915 and 1922 within the existing framework of the 18th Century Parkland setting. The gardens have undergone an extensive programme of restoration with new plantings rich in variety and interest. Gardens are not static and Kingston Maurward, like all good gardens, is constantly evolving.

The Animal Park is a firm favourite with children and home to an interesting collection of animals. There is a large play area and plenty of space for picnics. The Visitor Centre provides information on the Animal Park and Gardens and has a wide variety of plants and gifts for sale.

Fact File

Opening Times: 5th January to 19th December 10am to 5.30pm.
Admission Rates: Adults £4.00, Senior Citizen £4.00, Child £2.50
Groups Rates: Minimum group size: 10
Adults £3.50, Senior Citizen £3.50, Child £2.50
Facilities: Visitor Centre, Shop, Tea Room, Plant Sales, Picnic Area, Children's Play Area, Animal Park.
Disabled Access: Yes. Toilet and parking for disabled on site. Wheelchairs on loan, booking necessary.
Tours/Events: Guided walks are available if booked in advance.
Special events take place throughout the year, telephone for details.
Coach Parking: Yes
Length of Visit: Minimum 2 hours
Booking Contact: Ginny Rolls
Kingston Maurward, Dorchester, Dorset, DT2 8PY
Telephone: 01305 215003   Fax: 01305 215001
Email: events@kmc.ac.uk
Website: www.kmc.ac.uk
Location: Signposted from the roundabout at the eastern end of the Dorchester by-pass A35.

Please quote this guide when booking

Stapehill is a superb venue for group visits, offering a wide range of attractions to suit people of all tastes and ages for one admission price. The glorious award winning gardens, including the stunning Japanese Garden stocked with beautiful koi carp are a joy to behold. The 12,000 sq. ft museum with it's artisan workshops tells the history of farming through Victorian England. The 19th Century Cistercian Abbey houses the crafts people and has the Nuns Chapel, Cloisters and Cloister Garden plus the history of the Abbey, all this creates a truly unique experience, and with all but the gardens under cover, even the weather cannot spoil a memorable day at Stapehill.

The lovely licensed coffee shop provides morning coffee, light lunches, afternoon, and cream teas. Special events are held throughout the year including craft fairs, flower and garden festival and our magical Christmas weekends.

Fact File

Opening Times: Daily 10am - 5pm Easter - September. Wednesday - Sunday 10am - 4pm October - Easter. Closed Christmas Holiday and all of January.

Admission Rates: Adults £7.50, Senior Citizen £7.00, Child £4.50

Groups Rates: Minimum group size: 15
Adults £6.00, Senior Citizen £5.50, Child £4.00

Facilities: Visitor Centre, Shop, Plant Sales, Teas, Licensed Coffee Shop with homemade quiches and other light lunches.

Disabled Access: Yes. Toilet and parking for disabled on site.

Tours/Events: All year - please call for details.

Coach Parking: Yes

Length of Visit: 2 1/2 plus hours (all weather attraction)

Booking Contact: Mrs Sheena Tinsdale. Stapehill Abbey, 276 Wimborne Road West, Stapehill, Wimborne, Dorset, BH21 2EB. Telephone: 01202 861686 Fax: 01202 894589

Email: None

Website: None

Location: 2 1/2 miles east of the Historic town of Wimborne Minster.
Just off A31 at Canford Bottom roundabout.

Please quote this guide when booking

The garden is a highly individual creation of Sir Frederick Gibberd, master planner for Harlow new town. It is sited on the side of a small valley which slopes down to a brook. Occupying some seven acres, the garden was planned as a series of 'rooms', each with its own character. The glades, pools and alleys provide settings for some fifty sculptures, large ceramic pots, architectural salvage, a gazebo and even a children's moated castle with a drawbridge! Jane Brown, the garden and landscape design writer, has described it as "one of the few outstanding examples of 20th Century garden design"

The Gibberd Garden Trust aims to realise Sir Frederick's wish that the garden should be open to the public for study and relaxation. It has been acquired with the generous help of the Heritage Lottery Fund and is currently undergoing an imaginative and extensive restoration programme.

Fact File

Opening Times: 2pm to 6pm Wednesdays, Saturdays, Sundays & Bank Holidays.
Beginning April to end September.
Admission Rates: Adults £4.00, Concessions £2.50, Child Free if accompanied
Groups Rates: Minimum group size: 10 (As above during open times).
One free entry in 10. Please telephone for details at other times.
Facilities: Visitor Centre, Shop, Teas.
Disabled Access: Restricted. Toilet and parking for disabled on site.
Tours/Events: None.
Coach Parking: Please telephone to make arrangements (restricted access, 33 seater only).
Length of Visit: 2 hours
Booking Contact: Mrs Jane Quinton
The Gibberd Garden, Marsh Lane, Gilden Way, Harlow, Essex, CM17 0NA
Telephone: 01279 442112
Email: None
Website: www.thegibberdgarden.co.uk
Location: Off B183 Harlow to Hatfield Heath Road. Brown signs.

Please quote this guide when booking

RHS Garden Hyde Hall is truly a garden of its time. Set on a hilltop amongst rolling hills of arable crops, the garden combines environmental and sustainable practices with the high standards of horticulture for which the RHS gardens are renown.

The widely praised and award winning Dry Garden showcases the plants and growing techniques that can be employed in a garden that receives no artificial irrigation, using low intervention methods.

Hyde Hall is managed with biodiversity in mind, and this has led to the creation of two wildflower meadows and, new for 2004, a model 'Garden for Wildlife' designed to demonstrate gardening for wildlife on a domestic scale.

Fact File

Opening Times:	Now open all year (except for Christmas Day)
	10am to 6pm (5pm or dusk October -March) last entry 1 hour before closing.
Admission Rates:	Adults £4.50, Child £1.00
Groups Rates:	Minimum group size: 10 pre-booked
	Adults £3.50, Free meal voucher for coach driver.
Facilities:	Plant Centre & Gift Shop, Licensed Barn Restaurant, Visitor Centre, Garden Library.
Disabled Access:	Most areas. Toilet and parking for disabled on site. Ramped access to Barn Restaurant.
Tours/Events:	Guided tours by special arrangement only.
	On-going Programme of Events throughout the year, including Summer Festival Fortnight, Apple Festival and Rose Weekend. Contract the garden for a copy of Events Programme.
Coach Parking:	Yes
Length of Visit:	3 - 4 hours
Booking Contact:	Jane Kernan. RHS Garden Hyde Hall, Buckhatch Lane, Rettendon, Chelmsford, Essex, CM3 8ET. Telephone: 01245 400256 Fax: 01245 402100
Email:	hydehall@rhs.org.uk
Website:	www.rhs.org.uk
Location:	South-east of Chelmsford, Brown tourism signed from A130 bypass at Rettendon.

Please quote this guide when booking

The newly redesigned Walled Garden at Marks Hall was greeted with great enthusiasm when it opened in 2003.

The five individual gardens and the double long border are a unique blend of traditional and contemporary, combining unusual landscaping and creative and colourful planting. This garden is at its best from early summer through to autumn but on the opposite lake bank there is the Millennium Walk designed to be at its best in the shortest days of the year. Here the stems of dogwood, rubus and birch reflect in the lake and the scent of Hamamelis lingers.

There is much more to see in this Arboretum and Garden of over 100 acres and new plantings mature and surprise each year.

Fact File

Opening Times:	Tuesday - Sunday 10.30am - 5pm, Bank Holidays and winter weekends.
Admission Rates:	£3.50 per car
Groups Rates:	Minimum group size: 12
	£1.50 per person
Facilities:	Visitor Centre, Shop, Plant Sales, Teas, Restaurant.
Disabled Access:	Yes. Toilet and parking for disabled on site. Wheelchairs and buggy on loan.
Tours/Events:	Please telephone for details.
Coach Parking:	Yes
Length of Visit:	2 1/2 hours minimum
Booking Contact:	Marian Ripper
	Marks Hall, Coggeshall, Essex, CO6 1TG
	Telephone: 01376 563796 Fax: 01376 563132
Email:	anyone@markshall.org.uk
Website:	www.markshall.org.uk
Location:	Signed from A120 Coggeshall by pass.

Please quote this guide when booking

Batsford Arboretum & Wild Garden - The Cotswolds Secret Garden.

One of the largest private collection of trees in Great Britain. See spring flowers as they cascade down the hillside. Many wild orchids and fritillaries adorn the arboretum. In autumn the many rare and unusual trees explode into their magnificent reds, golds and purples.

Follow the stream through pools and waterfalls to its source, make a wish with the giant Buddha. Find the Foo Dog hidden amongst the trees, then negotiate the waterfall without getting too wet. See if you can find Algernon and Clementine on the lake, then rest awhile and view the deer in the Deer Park. Fifty acres of peace, tranquillity - pure Cotswold magic!

Fact File

Opening Times:	10am - 5pm 1st February - 15th November.
	Week-ends only from 15th November - 1st February.
	Also open Boxing Day & New Years Day.
Admission Rates:	Adults £5.00, Senior Citizen £4.00, Child £1.00
Groups Rates:	Minimum group size: 12. Admission Rates less 10%.
Facilities:	Visitor Centre, Shop, Plant Sales, Teas, Restaurant, Garden Centre, Falconry Centre, Reptile Rescue.
Disabled Access:	Partial. Toilet and parking for disabled on site. Wheelchairs on loan, booking necessary.
Tours/Events:	Tours by arrangement. Events to be arranged.
Coach Parking:	Yes
Length of Visit:	2 hours
Booking Contact:	Mr Chris Pilling
	Batsford Arboretum, Batsford Park, Moreton in Marsh, Glos, GL56 9QB.
	Telephone: 01386 701441 Fax: 01386 701829
Email:	batsarb@batsfound.freeserve.co.uk
Website:	www.batsford-arboretum.co.uk
Location:	1 mile east of Morton in Marsh on A44 road.

Please quote this guide when booking

The six acres of garden surrounding this Cotswolds manor house which was remodelled by Inigo Jones in 1636 offer many varied features and surprises. Huge Rhododendron borders (the only ones in the Cotswolds) greet the visitor. Rhododendrons are in flower from Christmas to the late autumn. The trees are either mature, dating from 1850 - Scots Pines, Wellingtonias, Douglas Firs, Copper Beeches etc - or Cedars, Paulownias, over 30 Magnolias, collections of Stuartias, Nothofagus and Eucryphias and countless Acers planted from 1960.

There is a Japanese Garden, a Himalayan Garden with Moutan Tree Paeonies (p.suffruticosa) a Secret Garden with many rare species, a Rose Garden and a Catalpa Walk. The Victorian Kitchen Garden shelters a Vineyard planted in 2000 and a Palm Garden planted in 2002 with Washingtonia, Trachycarpus and Mexican Blue Palms plus Olive Trees and Cypresses and Cordylines.

Fact File

Opening Times:	For charity (NGS) Sunday 30th May 2pm - 6pm. Groups by appointment only May - October.
Admission Rates:	Adults £3.00, Senior Citizen £3.00, Child £1.50. (NGS day only)
Groups Rates:	Minimum group size: 15
	Adults £5.00, Senior Citizen £5.00, Child £1.50. (Guided tours by owner)
Facilities:	Teas, Plant Stall on 30th May. For groups by appointment.
Disabled Access:	Yes. Toilet and parking for disabled on site.
Tours/Events:	Sculpture Park Project 15th May to 6th June. Wine tastings from our Vineyard.
Coach Parking:	Yes
Length of Visit:	1 - 2 hours
Booking Contact:	Mr or Mrs Hamish Cathie
	Barton House, Barton-On-The-Heath, Moreton-In-Marsh, Glos, GL56 0PJ
	Telephone: 01608 674303 Fax: 01608 674365
Email:	None
Website:	None
Location:	Between Moreton-in-Marsh and Chipping Norton off A44 (Evesham - Oxford Road),
	Turn at sign "Barton 1 1/4 ".

Please quote this guide when booking

Intensively planted, this 3-acre garden features excitingly planted herbaceous borders full of stunning plant and colour combinations.

Neatly clipped box and yew is found in knots, parterres and spiralling topiary. Water wends its way through small fountains, pools and ponds. A sub-tropical border, raised alpine troughs, a shadehouse, all provide further variety in this continually evolving garden. And add to the whole, a myriad of magically planted pots and containers.

Planted less than 10 years ago with a wide variety of trees, the seven-acre field opposite already boasts some sizeable specimens.

The imposing 16th century Tithe barn now houses a gallery of contemporary Art, Craft and Design.

Fact File

Opening Times: 26th May - 31st August: Wednesday, Thursday & Friday. September & October Thursday & Friday only. 10am - 5pm.

Admission Rates: Adults £4.50, Senior Citizen £4.00, Child Free

Groups Rates: Minimum group size: 20
Adults £4.00, Senior Citizen £4.00, Child Free

Facilities: Gallery of Contemporary Art, Craft, Design in the Tithe Barn, Teas & Light Meals, Unusual Plants for Sale.

Disabled Access: There is limited Access for wheelchairs.

Tours/Events: None

Coach Parking: Yes

Length of Visit: 1 1/2 hours

Booking Contact: Monique B Paice
Bourton House, Bourton-On-The-Hill, Moreton-in-Marsh, Glos, GL56 9AE
Telephone: 01386 700121 Fax: 01386 701081

Email: cd@bourtonhouse.com

Website: www.bourtonhouse.com

Location: 2 miles west of Moreton-in-Marsh on the A44.

Please quote this guide when booking

Hidcote Manor Garden is one of England's great Arts and Craft gardens. Created by the American horticulturist Major Lawrence Johnston in 1907, Hidcote is famous for its rare trees and shrubs, outstanding herbaceous borders and unusual plants from all over the world.

The garden is divided by tall hedges and walls to create a series of outdoor 'rooms' each with its own special and unique character. From the formal splendour of the White Garden and Bathing Pool to the informality and beauty of the Old Garden, visitors are assured of a surprise around every corner.

The numerous outdoor rooms reach their height at different times of the year, making a visit to Hidcote Manor Garden enjoyable whatever the season.

Fact File

Opening Times: 27 March - 31 October: Monday, Tuesday, Wednesday, Saturday & Sunday 10.30am - 6pm (Last admission 5pm) from 3 October last admission 4pm.

Admission Rates: Adults £6.20, Senior Citizen £6.20, Child £3.10

Groups Rates: Minimum group size: 15
Adults £5.60, Senior Citizen £5.60, Child £2.50

Facilities: Shop, Plant Sales, Teas, Restaurant.

Disabled Access: Partial. Toilet and parking for disabled on site. Wheelchairs on loan.

Tours/Events: Please contact the property for a list of special events.

Coach Parking: Yes. Groups must book in advance.

Length of Visit: 2 hours

Booking Contact: Lisa Edinborough
Hidcote Manor Garden, Hidcote Bartrim, Chipping Campden, Glos, GL55 6LR
Telephone: 01386 438333 Fax: 01386 438817

Email: hidcote@nationaltrust.org.uk

Website: www.nationaltrust.org.uk/hidcote

Location: 4 miles north east of Chipping Campden; 8 miles south of Stratford upon Avon & signposted from B4632 Stratford/Broadway road, close to the village of Micheleton.

Please quote this guide when booking

The 6 acres of garden surrounding Hodges Barn, a converted 15th century Columbarium, are all intensively planted. The terraces, courtyards and gardens are all divided into rooms surrounded either by walls or hedges. Roses scramble everywhere and are planted in large borders underplanted with bulbs and campanulas to give year round interest. The herbaceous border is formal and contains some plants which are old fashioned favourites, some rarely seen in gardens elsewhere. The stagnant 'Stew Pond' water garden is surrounded by water loving plants and this leads the visitor into a woodland area. The grass is left long in here and the mown paths wend through the interesting collection of ornamental trees carpeted in spring by daffodils and bluebells. Harmony and variety are the essential qualities of this garden.

Fact File

Opening Times:	18/19th April, 23rd/24th May, 6th, 7th & 9th July and by appointment.
Admission Rates:	Adults £5.00, Senior Citizen £5.00, Child Free
Facilities:	Light Lunches and Teas available if ordered before visit.
Disabled Access:	Yes. Parking for disabled on site.
Tours/Events:	Shipton Moyne village gardens Open Day 20th June, teas in village hall.
Coach Parking:	Yes
Length of Visit:	1 - 1 1/2 hours
Booking Contact:	Mrs Amanda Hornby
	Hodges Barn, Shipton Moyne, Tetbury, Glouestershire, GL8 8PR
	Telephone: 01666 880202 Fax: 01666 880373
Email:	None
Website:	None
Location:	1 mile from Tetbury on A433, turn left to Shipton Moyne.
	1/4 mile on Malmesbury side of village, cattlegrid on left, long drive.

Please quote this guide when booking

Kiftsgate Rose

We gardeners all make mistakes and we usually learn to live with them. Some of my most successful planting combinations have come about by forgetting what was there last year and popping a new plant into an apparently empty spot and then discovering a striking or harmonious combination emerges. Our largest mistake however is the Kiftsgate rose. Its huge form gives a stunning cascade of white flowers in July but it started out in life as a case of mistaken identity.

The original plant, which has now embraced three trees here at Kiftsgate Court in Gloucestershire, was planted in the 1930s by my grandmother Heather Muir as a Moschata rose. She had bought it from E A Bunyard, a nurseryman and plant breeder. It was left to grow unchecked through the war and it was only when that great rose expert Graham Stuart Thomas visited Kiftsgate in the late 1940s that this rose was identified as a particularly vigorous form of Rosa filipes and was named after the garden. Bunyard had died in the meantime and with him any record of his choice of parents for this monster.

Seventy years on, the original plant flourishes at 20 metres high and 25 metres along the Rose Border. Left unchecked it would continue its trifid like advance and only our annual hack stops it swamping all its neighbours. For anyone wanting to plant a Kiftsgate rose my advice is Beware! It can lift the roof off your house as it did for one of our neighbours or bar you from your garage. But, find a spot where there is plenty of room and a suitable host like an old apple tree and Kiftsgate will flourish and reward you with a magnificent flowering display in summer followed by a good show of hips in the autumn.

Although it will sometimes flower in its first year, do not be surprised if it takes four or five years. During this time it will be growing vigorously towards the light and won't bother to waste its energy on flowering. Only when it emerges above its host will it start to flower profusely and reward your patience.

Mistake it may be, but its one I could never be without.

Anne Chambers

Kiftsgate is a glorious garden to visit throughout the seasons with spectacular views to the Malvern Hills and beyond. Three generations of women gardeners have designed, planted and sustained this garden.

The upper gardens around the house are planted to give harmonious colour schemes, whilst the sheltered lower gardens recreate the atmosphere of warmer countries. The latest addition is a modern water garden which provides an oasis of tranquillity and contrast to the exuberance of the flower gardens.

On open days plants grown from the garden are for sale. A wide and interesting selection are always available. The tearoom in the house offers delicious home made cream teas and light lunches in June and July.

Fact File

Opening Times:	April, May, August, September - Wednesday, Thursday & Sunday 2pm - 6pm.
	June & July - Monday, Wednesday, Thursday, Saturday & Sunday 12 noon - 6pm.
Admission Rates:	Adults £5.00, Senior Citizen £5.00, Child £1.50
Groups Rates:	Coaches by appointment, 20 adults and more £4.50 per person.
Facilities:	Plants For Sale, Tea Room.
Disabled Access:	No.
Tours/Events:	None.
Coach Parking:	Yes
Length of Visit:	1 1/2 hours
Booking Contact:	Mrs Anne Chambers
	Kiftsgate Court Garden, Chipping Campden, Gloucestershire, GL55 6LN
	Telephone: 01386 438777 Fax: 01386 438777
Email:	kiftsgte@aol.com
Website:	www.kiftsgate.co.uk
Location:	3 miles north east of Chipping Campden. Follow signs towards Mickleton, then follow brown tourist signs to Kiftsgate Court Gardens.

Please quote this guide when booking

Mill Dene Garden surrounds an old Cotswold stone water-mill dating back to Norman times and is set in its own steeply sided valley. The garden has been designed and planted by the owner, Wendy Dare.

The garden seems to have evolved naturally in typical 'english country garden' relaxed style. From the tranquil mill-pond, stream and grotto at the bottom of the garden (with frost pocket and bog garden) steep terraces rise along terraces with a trompe l'oeil to tease the eye and old and huge standard Sanders White Roses with lavender at their feet which look at their best June/July. On the next level is the Cricket lawn with high Summer borders and at the very top of the garden backed by the village Church and with views over the Cotswolds hills, are the Fantasy Fruit garden and the Potager.

A garden made from a field not long ago offers challenges of a north facing and shady site cleverly overcome.

Fact File

Opening Times: 4th April - 29th October, Tuesday to Friday, weekends by appointment only.
Sundays 2pm - 6pm during exhibitions only.

Admission Rates: Adults £4.00, Senior Citizen £3.75, Child £1.00

Groups Rates: Minimum group size: 20 - Adults £3.75

Facilities: Unusual Plant Sales, Group Refreshments by arrangement.

Disabled Access: Partial. Parking for disabled on site by arrangement only.

Tours/Events: Introductory talk - 10 -15 minutes £25. Guided tour by owner £100.
Poetry and prose carved in wood, glass, slate and stone by some of the UK's best letter cutters, set in this beautiful garden to give visitors ideas for their own gardens; June & July.

Coach Parking: Nearby (Limited parking for 10 cars).

Length of Visit: 1 1/2 hours

Booking Contact: Mrs Wendy Dare. Mill Dene, Blockley, Moreton-in-Marsh, Gloucestershire, GL56 9HU
Telephone: 01386 700457 Fax: 01386 700526

Email: wendy@milldene.co.uk   **Website:** www.gardenvisit-cotswolds.co.uk

Location: Take the Blockley turn off the A44 at Bourton on the Hill <u>only</u>.
Following brown signs, stop at 1st left left turn behind village gates by School Lane, and unload, then park in the village sports ground.

Please quote this guide when booking

This lovely timeless English garden, which commands spectacular views over the Golden Valley has most of the features one would expect a garden started in the 17th century. There are extensive yew hedges and a notable yew walk dividing the walled garden, the york stone terrace, the Lutyens Loggia overhung with Wisteria, and a good specimen of magnolia sulangiana. The south lawn supports splendid grass steps and a fine mulberry (probably planted when the original house was built in 1620). West of the house the ground descends a series of grassed terraces and shrubberies. Within the walled garden are two good herbaceous borders, amongst the longest in the country. The walls are planted with climbing and rambler roses and there is a rose pergola dividing the border. A rill with a fountain and the stone summer-house were added as a feature to mark the new Millennium. More recently a circular parterre has been established with tulips, alliums, hebes and lavender. There are many fine specimen trees and the spring show of blossom and bulbs is notable.

Fact File

Opening Times:	10am - 5pm, Tuesday, Wednesday & Thursday, 1st April - 30th September.
Admission Rates:	Adults £3.50, Senior Citizen £3.50, Child Free
Groups Rates:	Minimum group size: 20
	Adults £3.15, Senior Citizen £3.15, Child Free
Facilities:	Nurseries Adjacent.
Disabled Access:	Yes. Parking for disabled on site.
Tours/Events:	None.
Coach Parking:	Yes
Length of Visit:	1 1/2 hours
Booking Contact:	Major M.T.N.H. Wills
	Misarden Park, Miserden, Stroud, Glos, GL6 7JA
	Telephone: 01285 821303 Fax: 01285 821530
Email:	None
Website:	None
Location:	Follow signs to Miserden from A417 or from B4070.

Please quote this guide when booking

Historic formal hillside garden, Stuart period. The Tudor manor house (1450-1616), garden and outbuildings lie in a picturesque wooded setting under the Cotswold hills.

The terraced garden is a rare survival of an early formal garden on a manorial scale, re-ordered in 1723, with magnificent yew topiary, old roses and box parterres. After being uninhabited for over 100 years, it was restored sympathetically in 'Old English' style by Norman Jewson in 1926.

Fact File

Opening Times: 1st April to 30th September, Tuesdays to Sundays and Bank Holiday Mondays.
Admission Rates: Adults £4.80, Senior Citizen £4.80, Child £2.00
Groups Rates: Minimum group size: 15
Adults £4.50, Senior Citizen £4.50, Child £2.00
Facilities: Restaurant, Lunches and Teas.
Disabled Access: No. Parking for disabled on site.
Tours/Events: None.
Coach Parking: Yes
Length of Visit: 1 1/2 - 2 hours
Booking Contact: Julia Webb
Owlpen Manor, Uley, Dursley, Gloucestershire, GL11 5BZ
Telephone: 01453 860261 Fax: 01453 860819
Email: sales@owlpen.com
Website: www.owlpen.com
Location: 1/2 mile east off B4066 at village green in Uley, between Dursley and Stroud.

Please quote this guide when booking

Painswick Rococo Garden is a fascinating insight into 18th century English garden design. The only complete Rococo garden in England, it dates from a brief period (1720 - 1760) when English gardens where changing from the formal to the informal. These Rococo gardens combined formal vistas with winding woodland walks and more natural planting. However Rococo gardens were so much more, their creators showed off their wealth and included features that were both flamboyant and frivolous. The gardens featured buildings of unusual architectural styles, to be used as both eye catchers and view points. These gardens became regency playrooms, an extension of the house to be enjoyed by the owner and his guests.

We are restoring the Garden back to how it was shown in a painting dated 1748. We have contemporary buildings, woodland walks, herbaceous borders, and a large kitchen garden all hidden away in a charming Cotswold valley with splendid views of the surrounding countryside.

Fact File

Opening Times:	10th January - 31st October. Daily 11am - 5pm.
Admission Rates:	Adults £4.00, Senior Citizen £3.50, Child £2.00
Groups Rates:	Minimum group size: 20 (Includes free introductory talk)
	Adults £3.50, Senior Citizen £3.50
Facilities:	Visitor Centre, Shop, Plant Sales, Teas, Restaurant.
Disabled Access:	No. Toilet for disabled on site.
Tours/Events:	None
Coach Parking:	Yes
Length of Visit:	2 hours
Booking Contact:	Paul Moir
	Painswick Rococo Garden, Painswick, Gloucestershire, GL6 6TH
	Telephone: 01452 813204 Fax: 01452 814888
Email:	prm@rococogarden.co.uk
Website:	www.rococogarden.co.uk
Location:	1/2 mile outside Painswick on B4073.

The garden was laid out (1909-1929) as a series of outdoor rooms covering about 8 acres. Each garden room has a different character and is bounded by either walls or hedges.

The Leisure Garden has 26 separate beds with a wide variety of planting dominated by yellow shrubs and roses. There is a collection of stone troughs with alpines as well a Rockery with bigger alpines. The White Borders start the year with many different snowdrops. Topiary is a feature of the garden with extensive yew, box, beech and holly hedges and clipped features. The Herbaceous Borders are magnificent, peaking late June but with plenty flowering into September. Many different types of roses flourish in the garden including old fashioned well-scented ones. There is a walled Kitchen Garden which has other plants besides vegetables including trained apples and pears.

Fact File

Opening Times: 8th, 12th and 15th February from 1.30pm.
Wednesday, Saturday & Bank Holidays 3rd May - 30th August, 2pm-5pm (House & Garden).
Mondays June - July, 2pm-5pm (Garden only).

Admission Rates: Adults £4.00, Senior Citizen £4.00, Child £1.00 (5-15yrs) (Garden only).

Facilities: Teas, Wednesday, Saturday & Bank Holidays.

Disabled Access: Yes. Parking for disabled on site.

Tours/Events: House also open.

Coach Parking: Yes

Length of Visit: 1 plus hours

Booking Contact: Simon Biddulph
Rodmarton Manor, Rodmarton, Cirencester, Gloucestershire, GL7 6PF
Telephone: 01285 841253 Fax: 01285 841298

Email: simon.biddulph@farming.co.uk

Website: www.rodmarton-manor.co.uk

Location: Off A433 between Cirencester and Tetbury.

Please quote this guide when booking

Surrounding Sudeley Castle are 14 acres of glorious gardens, which won the HHA/Christies 'Garden of the Year Award' in 1996. Designed almost as a continuation of the Castle, ten smaller individual gardens blend seamlessly together. Bold areas of planting such as those surrounding the spectacular 15th Century Tithe Barn ruins contrast with intricate detail as seen in the Tudor Knot Garden. Topiary features strongly throughout and the famous Queens Garden, full of old fashioned roses, is furnished on two sides by magnificent double yew hedges planted in 1860. All of the gardens are managed using organic principles and a Heritage Seed Library Garden, laid out as a Victorian Kitchen Garden, works in conjunction with the HDRA to help preserve rare and traditional varieties of vegetable. New for 2004, the East Garden with its eastern influences will create a peaceful area to reflect on the beautiful surroundings.

Fact File

Opening Times: Gardens - 6th March until 31st October 2004.
Castle - 27th March until 31st October 2004.

Admission Rates: Gardens only - Adults £5.50 - £6.50, Senior Citizen £4.50 - £5.50, Child £3.25 - £4.25

Groups Rates: Minimum group size: 20
Castle and Gardens - Adults £5.85, Senior Citizen £4.85, Child £3.85

Facilities: Visitor Centre, Shop, Plant Sales, Teas, Adventure Playground, Picnic Area.

Disabled Access: Limited - gardens only. Toilet and parking for disabled on site.
Wheelchairs on loan (subject to availability).

Tours/Events: Guided tours available (must be pre-booked).
Special events programme please telephone for details.

Coach Parking: Yes   **Length of Visit:** 3 hours

Booking Contact: Natalie Dyke
Sudeley Castle, Winchcombe, Cheltenham, Gloucestershire, GL54 5JD
Telephone: 01242 602308   Fax: 01242 602959

Email: marketing@sudeley.org.uk

Website: www.sudeleycastle.co.uk

Location: On B4632, 8 miles north east of Cheltenham.

Please quote this guide when booking

Westonbirt is a wonderful world of trees and is beautiful at any time of year. Set in 600 acres of glorious Cotswold countryside, it has 17 miles of paths along which to stroll and over 18,000 numbered trees, including 100 champions - the oldest, largest, tallest of that species in the country.

In spring it is ablaze with colour from rhododendrons, azaleas, magnolias and bluebells, but is more famous for its autumn colour, when it seems almost every tree turns a brilliant red, orange or gold. Summer brings cool leafy glades where butterflies and bees busily collect nectar, and an exciting events programme including The Festival of the Garden and The Festival of Wood. Add to this a restaurant, shop and plant centre and you have a perfect day out.

Fact File

Opening Times: 10am - 8pm or dusk if earlier.
Admission Rates: Adults £6.00 (£7.50 4th June - 5th Sept), Senior Citizen £5.00 (£6.50), Child £1.00
Groups Rates: Please telephone for details.
Facilities: Shop, Plant Sales, Café, Restaurant.
Disabled Access: Yes. Toilet and parking for disabled on site. Wheelchairs on loan, booking necessary.
Tours/Events: The Festival of the Garden - 4th June - 5th September.
Festival of Wood - August, Enchanted Wood - November/December, Summer Concerts.
Coach Parking: Yes
Length of Visit: 2 - 3 hours
Booking Contact: Helen Daniels
Westonbirt Arboretum, Tetbury, Gloucestershire, GL8 8QS
Telephone: 01666 880220 Fax: 01666 880559
Email: westonbirt@forestry.gsi.gov.uk
Website: www.forestry.gov.uk/westonbirt
Location: 3 miles south west of Tetbury on A433.

Please quote this guide when booking

Exbury Gardens & Steam Railway   Hampshire

Natural beauty is in abundance at Exbury Gardens, a 200-acre woodland garden on the east bank of the Beaulieu River. Created by Lionel de Rothschild in the 1920's, the Gardens are a stunning vision of his inspiration. The spring displays of rhododendrons, azaleas, camellias and magnolias are world famous. The daffodil meadow, rock garden, rose garden, herbaceous grasses garden, ponds and cascades ensure year round interest. Exbury is a previous winner of Christie's Garden of the Year.

Newly opened is the Exbury Gardens Railway. Why not 'let the train take the strain' on a 1 1/4 mile journey over a bridge, through a tunnel, across a pond in the Summer Lane Garden planted with bulbs, herbaceous perennials and grasses? Then travel along the top of the rock garden and across a viaduct into the American Garden.

Fun for all the family and a day out at Exbury that the weather cannot spoil.

Fact File

Opening Times:	1st March to 31st October daily 10am - 5.30pm.
	6th November to 19th December weekends 10am - 4pm.
Admission Rates:	(2003 Rates).
	Adults £3.50/£5.50, Senior Citizen £3.00/£5.00, Child (10-15) £2.50/£3.50 under 10's free
Groups Rates:	Minimum group size: 15
	Adults £5.00, Senior Citizen £5.00
Facilities:	Gift Shop, Plants Sales, Teas, Restaurant, Buggy Tours.
Disabled Access:	Yes. Toilet and parking for disabled on site. Wheelchairs on loan.
	Accessible carriages on train.
Tours/Events:	Please call for information on guided tours & 'Meet & Greets' by arrangement on
	023 80 891203. Please call for details of special events.
Coach Parking:	Yes **Length of Visit:** 2 - 3 hours
Booking Contact:	Barbara King. Exbury Gardens, Estate Office, Exbury, Southampton, Hants, SO45 1AZ.
	Telephone: 023 80 891203 Fax: 023 80 899940
Email:	victoriaexbury@aol.com
Website:	www.exbury.co.uk
Location:	Junction 2 of M27, follow A326 to Fawley, off B3054, 3 miles Beaulieu.

Please quote this guide when booking

Set in the heart of the New Forest at Minstead this delightful, informal garden was established in 1922 and offers extensive collections of azaleas and rhododendrons as well as Winter and Summer flowering trees and shrubs. The recently rebuilt heather shelter affords a shady retreat with views over the lake and to mark the Millennium a Sensory Garden was created on the top lawn with easy access for wheelchair users. Tree houses, log cabins and a willow weave tunnel entertain younger visitors. A wide variety of mainly local arts and crafts are displayed in the Craft Gallery where light refreshments including cream teas are available. There is also a monthly changing exhibition of paintings by local artists. Work in the gardens is carried out by young people with learning disabilities under the supervision of horticultural instructors from our sister organisation The Minstead Training Project.

Fact File

Opening Times:	Gardens: Daily (except Christmas Day & Boxing Day), 10am - 5pm.
	Gallery: Daily - March - October, 10am - 5pm.
Admission Rates:	Adults £3.50, Senior Citizen £2.80, Child £1.50
Groups Rates:	Minimum group size: 10
	Adults £3.15, Senior Citizen £2.50, Child £1.35
Facilities:	Shop, Plant Sales, Teas, Monthly Art Exhibitions.
Disabled Access:	Yes. Toilet for disabled on site. Wheelchairs on loan, booking advised.
Tours/Events:	Tours by prior arrangement.
Coach Parking:	Yes
Length of Visit:	1 1/2 - 2 hours
Booking Contact:	Mrs Maureen Cole
	Furzey Gardens, School Lane, Minstead, Nr Lundhurst, Hampshire, SO43 7GL
	Telephone: 02380 812464 Fax: 02380 812297
Email:	info@furzey-gardens.org
Website:	www.furzey-gardens.org
Location:	1/2 mile north M27/A31 junction off A337 to Lundhurst - OS Map ref SU 273114.

Please quote this guide when booking

I have learned during the past years what above all I want from a garden: this is tranquillity'. So said Ralph Dutton, 8th and last Lord Sherborne, of his garden at Hinton Ampner. In the 1930's he created one of the great gardens of the 20th century, a masterpiece of design based upon the bones of a Victorian garden, in which he united a formal layout with varied and informal planting in pastel shades. It is a garden of all year round interest with scented plants and magnificent vistas over the park and surrounding countryside.

The garden forms the link between the woodland and parkland planting and the house, which he remodelled into a small neo-Georgian manor house and which contains his very fine collection of paintings and furniture. It is all set within the rolling Hampshire landscape that he loved and understood so well.

Fact File

Opening Times:	April - September: Garden daily except Thursday & Friday, 12 noon - 5pm.
	House Tuesday & Wednesday only plus Saturday and Sunday in August, 1.30pm - 5pm.
Admission Rates:	Garden - £4.80, House & Garden - £5.80, Child 5 - 16 half price
Groups Rates:	Minimum group size: 15
	House & Garden £5.20, Child 5 - 16 half price
Facilities:	Tea Room, Light Lunches served 12 noon - 2pm.
Disabled Access:	Yes. Toilet and parking for disabled on site. Wheelchairs on loan.
Tours/Events:	Monthly 'Meet the Gardener' walks and occasional demonstrations.
Coach Parking:	Yes but must be pre booked.
Length of Visit:	2 hours
Booking Contact:	Janet Green
	Hinton Ampner Garden, Bramdean, Nr Alresford, Hampshire, SO24 0LA
	Telephone: 01962 771305 Fax: 01962 793101
Email:	hintonampner@nationaltrust.org.uk
Website:	www.nationaltrust.org.uk
Location:	On A272 mid way between Winchester and Petersfield.

Please quote this guide when booking

Mottisfont boasts thirty acres of landscaped grounds with sweeping lawns and magnificent trees, set amidst glorious countryside along the River Test.

The twelfth century Augustine priory is now a house of some note, containing delightful rooms such as the drawing room decorated by Rex Whistler in "trompe l'oeil" fantasy style. It also houses an interesting collection of 19th and early 20th century pictures donated by painter Derek Hill.

The extensive gardens were remodelled gradually during the 20th century. Norah Lindsay designed a parterre, Geofrey Jellicoe redesigned the north front with an avenue of pollarded limes and an octagon of yews, all combine to provide interest throughout the seasons. Graham Stuart Thomas designed the walled garden in 1972, with beds divided by attractive box hedges, to contain the NATIONAL COLLECTION of OLD FASHIONED ROSES, with over 300 varieties. It is at its best in mid June, but has plenty to interest visitors later in summer and autumn.

Fact File

Opening Times:	Please telephone the information line for details 01794 341220.
Admission Rates:	Adults £6.50, Senior Citizen £6.50, Child £3.00
Groups Rates:	Minimum group size: 12
	Every 6th visitor goes free.
Facilities:	Visitor Centre, Shop, Plant Sales, Teas, Restaurant.
Disabled Access:	Yes. Toilet and parking for disabled on site. Wheelchairs on loan.
Tours/Events:	None.
Coach Parking:	Yes
Length of Visit:	2 hours
Booking Contact:	Terry Lewis
	Mottisfont Abbey, Mottisfont, Nr Romsey, Hampshire, SO51 0LP
	Telephone: 01794 344018 Fax: 01794 341429
Email:	mottisfontabbey@nationaltrust.org
Website:	www.nationaltrust.org
Location:	Signposted off A3057, Romsey to Stockbridge road, 4 miles north of Romsey.

Please quote this guide when booking

Enrich your knowledge of the natural world and seek inspiration for your own garden on a journey of discovery through the landscaped features, woodlands and walkways of the Sir Harold Hillier Gardens. Established in 1953 by the distinguished plantsman Sir Harold Hillier, the magnificent collection of over 42,000 plants from temperate regions around the world grow in a mixture of formal and informal landscapes set in 180-acres of rolling Hampshire countryside. Open all year; there is a stunning display throughout the seasons with new and interesting aspects of the Collection unfolding each week. The Gardens hold 11 National Plant Collections, over 100 Champion Trees and a variety of garden features including the Gurkha Memorial Garden and the Winter Garden. In 2003, a new £3.5 million Visitor & Education Pavilion overlooking the plant collection and surrounding countryside opened to the public. The Pavilion features a stylish licensed restaurant with open-air terrace, Gift Shop and exhibition space. An on-site Plant Centre offers a superb range of plants.

Fact File

Opening Times:	Daily: 10.30am - 6pm or dusk if earlier. Open all year except Christmas Day and Boxing Day.
Admission Rates:	Adults £6.00, Senior Citizen £5.50, Child under 16 years free
Groups Rates:	Minimum group size: 10 - Adults £5.00
Facilities:	New £3.5 million Visitor & Education Pavilion, Open-air terrace and restaurant, Gift Shop, Plant Centre.
Disabled Access:	Yes. Toilet and parking for disabled on site. Wheelchairs on loan, booking advised.
Tours/Events:	Pre-booked guided tour with Curator, Botanist, Head Gardener and horticultural staff available by arrangement. Please telephone for details about Special Events.
Coach Parking:	Yes (Free)
Length of Visit:	2 - 4 hours
Booking Contact:	Group Bookings. Sir Harold Hillier Gardens, Jermyns Lane, Romsey, Hampshire, SO51 0QA Telephone: 01794 368787 Fax: 01794 368027
Email:	info@hilliergardens.org.uk
Website:	www.hilliergardens.org.uk
Location:	The Gardens are situated, 3 miles north-east of Romsey. M3/M27 (West) to Romsey town centre. At Romsey follow brown heritage signs to the Hillier Gardens off the A3090. Alternatively, the Gardens can be approached from the A3057 Andover direction.

Please quote this guide when booking

Nestling in a woodland corner of Hampshire is this ravishingly attractive 1720's manor house, where busts of gods, emperors and dukes look down from the walls onto two major gardens. The inner gardens, enclosed by eighteenth century walls, are all devoted to parterres. One is filled with water lillies, another is of classical design with box topiary and a third enacts the whimsy of *Alice in Wonderland* with the story's characters in ivy and box topiary surrounded by roses of red and white. The main walled garden is planted in subtle hues of mauve, plum and blue, contained in beds that have been faithfully restored to their original outlines. A decorative potager is centred around berry-filled fruit cages where herbs, flowers and unusual vegetables are designed into colourful patterns. All this is surrounded by a second garden, a remarkable neo-classical park studded with follies, birdcages and monuments.

West Green House is the only garden to have a whole 'Gardeners World' programme dedicated to itself.

Fact File

Opening Times: Open 1st April to 31st August, Thursday - Sunday and Bank Holiday Mondays.
September, Saturday and Sunday 11am - 5pm.

Admission Rates: Adults £5.00

Groups Rates: Groups by arrangement please telephone for details.

Facilities: Tea / Coffee Shop serving light lunches, Garden Shop.

Disabled Access: Yes. Toilet and parking for disabled on site.

Tours/Events: Plant Fair in May, Music Season - please telephone for details.
Special evenings including meals by arrangement.

Coach Parking: Yes

Length of Visit: 2 hours approximately

Booking Contact: West Green House, Thackhams Lane, West Green, Hartley Wintney, Hants, RG27 8JB
Telephone: 01252 845582 Fax: 01252 844611

Email: None

Website: None

Location: 10 miles north east of Basingstoke, 1 mile west of Hartley Wintney, 1 mile north of A30.

Please quote this guide when booking

From Spring bulbs to Autumn colour, this is a garden for all seasons. With over 60 champion trees and shrubs, the Gardens are recognised as "one of the best collections of plants held in private ownership", holding National Collections of Maples, Birches and Zelkovas. Rhododendrons and azaleas are spectacular in Spring, and the large kitchen garden with the long double herbaceous borders, Rose Garden and Spring Borders are always attractive. Autumn colours are superb.

Teas with local home-made food are available in the old dining-room. Rare and unusual plants are for sale, the majority grown in the garden, and there is a shop selling a wide range of gifts.

There are special entry rates for pre-booked groups of 20 or more people.

Fact File

Opening Times:	April - End of October, 12.30pm - 5.30pm excluding May & June 12noon - 6pm.
Admission Rates:	Adults £4.50, Senior Citizen £4.50, Child Free
Groups Rates:	Minimum group size: 20
	Adults £4.00, Senior Citizen £4.00, Child Free
Facilities:	Shop, Plant Sales, Teas.
Disabled Access:	Yes but limited to certain areas. Toilet and parking for disabled on site.
	Wheelchairs on loan, booking necessary.
Tours/Events:	Monday 3rd May Flower Fair, Sunday 17th October Plant Fair.
Coach Parking:	Yes
Length of Visit:	2 plus hours
Booking Contact:	Melanie Lloyd
	Hergest Croft Gardens, Kington, Herefordshire, HR5 3EG
	Telephone: 01544 230160 Fax: 01544 232031
Email:	gardens@hergest.co.uk
Website:	www.hergest.co.uk
Location:	Follow brown tourist signs off the A44 Rhayader.

Please quote this guide when booking

Hatfield House Gardens Hertfordshire

The Gardens at Hatfield House date from the early 17th century when Robert Cecil, 1st Earl of Salisbury, employed John Tradescant the Elder to plant and lay them out around his new home. Tradescant was sent to Europe where he found and brought back trees, bulbs, plants and fruit trees, which had never previously been grown in England.

These beautifully designed gardens included orchards, elaborate fountains, scented plants, water parterres, terraces, herb gardens and a foot maze. Following the fashion for landscape gardening and some neglect in the 18th century, restoration of these gardens started in earnest in Victorian times. The gardens to the west of the house, which include the Herb, Knot and Wilderness areas, can be seen when the house is open. However, all 42 acres, including the Kitchen Garden and the formal parterres to the East of the house leading down to the lake, are open on Fridays.

Fact File

Opening Times:	Easter Saturday - 30th September, 11am - 5.30pm.
Groups Rates:	Adults £4.50, Senior Citizen £4.50, Child £3.50 (Friday £6.50 - no concessions).
Facilities:	Shop, Tea Room, Restaurant, Gift Shop, Kiosk, Park Nature Trails.
Disabled Access:	Yes. Toilet and parking for disabled on site.
Tours/Events:	Flower Festival 11th - 13th June. Homes, Gardens, Flowers & Rare Breeds Show 3rd - 5th September.
Coach Parking:	Yes
Length of Visit:	2 1/2 hours
Booking Contact:	Assistant Administrator Hatfield House, Hatfield, Hertfordshire, AL9 5NQ Telephone: 01707 287010 Fax: 01707 287033
Email:	curator@hatfield-house.co.uk
Website:	www.hatfield-house.co.uk
Location:	21 miles north of London. M25 junction 23, seven miles. A1(M) junction 4 two miles. Signed off A414 and A1000. Opposite Hatfield Rail Station.

Please quote this guide when booking

Ventnor Botanic Garden Isle of Wight

Originally an offshoot of Hilliers Nursery, Ventnor Botanic Garden is devoted to exotic plants. It is not strictly a *botanic* garden, but it has a remarkable collection. Many of the plants - perhaps most - are from the southern hemisphere but flourish in the unique microclimate of the 'Undercliff' : widdringtonias from Zimbabwe and Tasmanian olearias, for instance, as well as astelias, *Sophora microphylla* and *Griselinia lucida* from New Zealand. *Geranium maderense* has naturalised on the sunny slopes and so has an amazing colony of 4m *Echium pininana*. Elsewhere are such Mediterranean natives as acanthus, cistus and *Coronilla valentina*, and a remarkable area called the Palm Garden, where stately foliage plants like yuccas, cordylines, phoriums and beschornerias are underplanted with watsonias, cannas and kniphofias. Almost destroyed by the gales of 1987 and 1990, the collections were rapidly re-made and the garden looks wonderfully vigorous again. 2001 saw some extensive re-landscaping of the Mediterranean Garden. The energetic head gardener has a splendid eye for planting. A magnificent Visitor Centre opened recently: It offers the venue for exhibitions, conferences and a programme of events as well as a restaurant for visitors. The nursery sells some very interesting and often tender plants.

Fact File

Opening Times:	Gardens all year round, dawn - dusk. Show-house & Plant Sales: 10am - 5pm daily, March - October, 10am - 4pm weekends, November - February. Visitor Centre: 10am - 6pm daily, March - October. 10am - 4pm weekends only, November - February.
Admission Rates:	Gardens, Visitor Centre and Plant Sales - free of charge. Show-house - small admission. Car parking charges apply.
Facilities:	Visitor Centre, 'Green House' Exhibition, Plant Sales, Gift Shop, Café, Conference & Function Facilities.
Disabled Access:	Yes. Toilet and parking for disabled on site. Wheelchairs on loan.
Tours/Events:	Please telephone for details.
Coach Parking:	Yes.
Length of Visit:	2 - 3 hours
Booking Contact:	Alison Ellsbury
	Ventnor Botanic Garden, Undercliff Drive, Ventnor, Isle of Wight, PO38 1UL
	Telephone: 01983 855397 Fax: 01983 856756
Email:	alison.ellsbury@iow.gov.uk
Website:	www.botanic.co.uk
Location:	Situated between Ventnor and St Lawrence on the A3055 coastal road.

Bedgebury Pinetum, situated in the High Weald of Kent, currently has the world's largest collection of temperate conifers on one site in the world. The diversity of colour and form of the conifers is amazing and there are 91 rare or endangered species being cared for as part of Bedgebury's worldwide conservation effort.

The Pinetum is a haven of tranquillity and peace set in beautiful parkland with lakes, streams, rolling hills and wide avenues. Every season has its own charm: a fall of snow creates a winter wonderland, there are carpets of bluebells flanked by magnificent rhododendrons and azaleas in spring, acres of wild flowers in summer, and shrubs and trees giving autumn colour, all set against the backdrop of the stunning conifers.

Fact File

Opening Times:	10am - 6pm Summer, 10am - 4pm Winter.
Admission Rates:	Adults £3.50, Senior Citizen £3.00, Child £1.50
Groups Rates:	Minimum group size: 20 plus less 10%, 40 plus less 20%
Facilities:	Visitor Centre, Shop, Teas and Light Snacks.
Disabled Access:	No. Parking for disabled on site.
Tours/Events:	Please telephone for details of events, list available from shop.
Coach Parking:	Yes
Length of Visit:	2 hours
Booking Contact:	Rosemary Mayhew
	Bedgebury Pinetum, Park Lane, Goudhurst, Nr Cranbrook, Kent, TN17 2SL
	Telephone: 01580 211781 Fax: 01580 212423
Email:	rosemary.mayhew@forestry.gsi.gov.uk
Website:	www.bedgeburypinetum.org.uk
Location:	Signposted from the A21, north of Flimwell on the B2079.

Please quote this guide when booking

There's magic and mystery, history and romance at this enchanting award-winning venue - which provides such an unusual combination of a traditional heritage garden with the contemporary landscaping of the ancient woodland.

First laid out in 1674 on a gentle, south-facing slope, the formal walled gardens are set against the romantic backdrop of a medieval moat, surrounding a classical Restoration manor house (not open to the public). They include herbaceous borders, an exquisite white rose garden with over 20 varieties of roses, a secret garden, knot garden, nut walk, paradise walk and oriental garden plus the drunken garden with its crazy topiary. And there's wonderful seasonal colour throughout spring, summer and autumn.

In complete contrast, in the ancient woodland of the 'Enchanted Forest' there are quirky and mysterious gardens developed by innovative designer, Ivan Hicks.

Fact File

Opening Times: 1st April - 5th November, daily 9.30am - 6pm (or dusk if earlier).

Admission Rates: Adults £8.50, Senior Citizen £7.20, Child (3-12yrs) £7.00, Family ticket (2+2) £28.50

Groups Rates: Minimum group size: 20
Adults £6.75, Senior Citizen from £5.00, Child £5.75

Facilities: Gift Shop, Licensed Restaurant, Plant Sales.

Disabled Access: Yes. Toilet and parking for disabled on site. Wheelchairs on loan.

Tours/Events: Guided tours for groups - pre booked only £25 per guide. Major programme of Special Events throughout the season, including a Midsummer Garden Celebration in June.

Coach Parking: Yes

Length of Visit: 3 - 4 hours

Booking Contact: Carrie Hare
Groombridge Place, Groombridge, Tunbridge Wells, Kent, TN3 9QG
Telephone: 01892 861444   Fax: 01892 863996

Email: office@groombridge.co.uk

Website: www.groombridge.co.uk

Location: 4 miles south west of Tunbridge Wells on B2110, just off the A264 between Tunbridge Wells and East Grinstead.

Please quote this guide when booking

The nine privately owned acres are remarkable for their variety and magnificent views, and against a backdrop of trees of outstanding shapes and contrast they include unusual topiary, water garden and arboretum, all set in the heart of a progressive fruit farm. Rose terraces enclosed by yew hedges slope down to a lake with a woodland area as a backdrop. The rock garden in a Japanese style and ornamented with stone lanterns and based on a series of pools follows an alternative gently winding route. Planting throughout is intensive giving colour and interest throughout the year.

The gardens have an atmosphere of peace and tranquillity with a wonderful contrast between the formal and informal. Restored from 1950 onwards, the gardens retain much of the original design of the early 1900s and offer a step back to more leisurely times with that magical charm of still being lived in.

Fact File

Opening Times:	Wednesday, Thursday, Saturday & Sunday 1pm - 5pm. Bank Holiday Mondays 11am - 5pm.
Admission Rates:	Adults £3.50, Senior Citizen £3.50, Child £1.00
Groups Rates:	Minimum group size: 10
	Adults £3.00, Senior Citizen £3.00, Child £1.00
Facilities:	Tea Room, Craft Centre (Sundays only), Small Gift Shop.
Disabled Access:	Yes, but difficult in places, sloped garden and steps in places.
	Toilet and parking for disabled on site.
Tours/Events:	Guided tours available £10 extra.
	Outdoor Shakespeare and Prom Concert in summer.
Coach Parking:	Yes
Length of Visit:	1 - 2 hours
Booking Contact:	Mrs L Dawes
	Mount Ephraim Gardens, Hernhill, Nr Faversham, Kent, ME13 9TX
	Telephone: 01227 751496 Fax: 01227 750940
Email:	sandys@freenetname.co.uk
Website:	www.mountephraimgardens.co.uk
Location:	Follow brown and white signs on A2 and A299. Just beyond end of M2.

Please quote this guide when booking

Penshurst Place & Gardens   Kent

Ancestral home of the Sidney family since 1552, with a history going back six and half centuries, Penshurst Place has been described as "the grandest and most perfectly preserved example of a fortified manor house in all England".

See the awe-inspiring Barons Hall with its 60ft high steeply angled roof and the State Rooms filled with fine tapestries, furniture, portraits and armour. The 11 acres of Gardens are as old as the original house - the walls and terraces were added in the Elizabethan era - and are divided into a series of self-contained garden rooms. Each garden room offers an abundance of variety in form, foliage and bloom and ensures a continuous display from Spring to Autumn.

There is also a Park with Woodland Trail, a Garden History Exhibition, a Toy Museum, Venture Playground, Shop, Plant Centre and Garden Tea Room, which contribute to a great day out.

Fact File

Opening Times:	Weekends from 6th March, Daily from 27th March - 31st October.
Admission Rates:	**House & Gardens,** Adults £7.00, Senior Citizen £6.50, Child £5.00
Groups Rates:	Minimum group size: 20
	Including garden tour, Adults £8.50, Senior Citizen £8.50, Child £4.50
Facilities:	Shop, Plant Sales, Teas.
Disabled Access:	Yes. Toilet and parking for disabled on site. Wheelchairs on loan, booking necessary.
Tours/Events:	Garden tour and Cream Tea - special offer for groups.
Coach Parking:	Yes
Length of Visit:	2 - 3 hours
Booking Contact:	Caroline Cole
	Penshurst Place, Penshurst, Kent, TN11 8DG
	Telephone: 01892 870307 Fax: 01892 870866
Email:	enquiries@penshurstplace.com
Website:	www.penshurstplace.com
Location:	M25 junction 5, follow A21 to Hastings. Exit at Hildenborough then follow brown tourist signs.

Please quote this guide when booking

Visit Scotney Castle and discover one of the most romantic gardens in England. The stunning ruins of the 14th century moated castle and its surrounding landscape were created in the 1830's by Edward Hussey III, resulting in one of the last and most successful expressions of the Picturesque movement.

From early in the year snowdrops, then swathes of primroses and daffodils cover the lawns by the moat and drifts of sweet smelling bluebells line the driveway. Magnificent azaleas, rhododendrons and Scotney's famous *Kalmia latifolia* follow and as Summer progresses we see the breath-taking fragrant white wisteria rambling the walls of the ruined castle. Finally the season comes to a close with rich autumnal hues of reds and gold's from liquidambars and Japanese Maples.

Why not stay a while longer and explore the 770 acres of beautiful ancient wood and parkland on our estate.

Fact File

Opening Times: Garden open - 20th March - 31st October.
Castle open May - September, 11am - 6pm, last entry 5pm Wednesday - Sunday.
Open Bank Holiday, closed on Good Friday.

Admission Rates: Adults £4.40, Senior Citizen £4.40, Child £2.20

Groups Rates: Minimum group size: 15, Wednesday - Friday only
Adults £3.80, Senior Citizen £3.80, Child £1.90

Facilities: Shop. Plant Sales (plant sales are as and when depending on the seasonal availability).

Disabled Access: Yes, but limited due to steep parts, map provided showing best route and photo album of Old Castle. Toilet and parking for disabled on site. Wheelchairs on loan.

Tours/Events: Garden tours available at extra cost.
Guided walks/garden tours, educational guided estate walks.

Coach Parking: Yes   **Length of Visit:** 1 1/2 - 2 hours

Booking Contact: Mr Pip Dodd. Scotney Castle, Lamberhurst, Nr Tunbridge Wells, Kent, TN3 8JN
Telephone: 01892 891081 Fax: 01892 890110

Email: scotneycastle@nationaltrust.org.uk   **Website:** www.nationaltrust.org.uk/scotneycastle

Location: 1 mile south of Lamberhurst on A21. Bus - Coastal Coach 256.
Station - Wadhurst (5 1/2 miles away) Free parking.

Please quote this guide when booking

Sissinghurst Castle Garden   Kent

Sissinghurst is a place that breathes old England, and yet the ideas behind its design, a series of intimate moments that together form a striking narrative - are very modern. Its Lime Walk, Herb Garden, Cottage Garden and above all the famous White Garden put on a kind of theatrical performance that marks the changing moods and colours of the seasons.

Vita Sackville-West and Harold Nicolson were an unusual couple - he a diplomat turned reviewer, she a writer and newspaper columnist who liked to work in a tower, not of ivory, but of warm pink brick.

Sissinghurst was originally built in the 1560's: once a poorhouse, and a prison, its Great Court was a ruin by the time the couple took it on in the 1930's. They built on the ancient template of a lost Elizabethan house to create a bold new story: the result is a triumphant essay in English style.

Fact File

Opening Times: 20th March to 31st October, Mondays, Tuesdays & Fridays 11am to 6.30pm.
Saturdays, Sunday & Bank Holidays 10am to 6.30pm. Closed Wednesdays & Thursdays.
Admission Rates: Adults £7.00, Family (2 adults 3 children) £17.50, Child £3.50, National Trust Members Free
Groups Rates: Minimum group size: 11 - Please telephone for details.
Facilities: Shop, Self Service Restaurant, Exhibition, Picnic Areas, Woodland Walks.
Disabled Access: Yes. Toilet and parking for disabled on site. Wheelchairs on loan, booking necessary.
Tours/Events: None
Coach Parking: Yes
Length of Visit: 2 1/2 hours
Booking Contact: Samantha Snaith
Sissinghurst Castle, Cranbrook, Kent, TN17 2AB
Telephone: 01580 710700   Fax: 01580 710702
Email: sissinghurst@nationaltrust.org.uk
Website: www.nationaltrust.org.uk/sissinghurst
Location: 2 miles north east of Cranbrook, 1 mile east of Sissinghurst village (A262).

Please quote this guide when booking

The garden surrounding Squerryes Court is beautiful throughout the seasons. In 1700 the garden was laid out in the formal style. When the Warde family acquired Squerryes in 1731, they swept away most of the formal garden and relandscaped it in the natural style then fashionable. The bones of the old garden survived.

Following the storm of 1987, the Warde family restored some of the formal garden using the 1719 print as a guideline. Hedges, pleached limes and a hornbeam avenue were planted. Box edged parterres containing lavender, santolina and purple sage were laid out. The Edwardian herbaceous borders were replanted. In other areas of the garden new borders have been created. The Victorian rockery features some fine topiary. The restoration is ongoing in the woodland garden, The lake, spring bulbs, rhododendrons and azaleas make this garden interesting all year. The manor house is also open.

Fact File

Opening Times: 1st April - 30th September, Wednesday, Thursday, Sunday & Bank Holiday Mondays. Garden open 12 noon, House open 1.30pm, last entry 5pm closes 5.30pm.

Admission Rates: House & Grounds Adults £5.00, Senior Citizen £4.40, Child £2.70 (under 14), Family £12.50 Grounds only Adults £3.40, Senior Citizen £2.90, Child £1.70 (under 14), Family £7.50

Groups Rates: Pre-booked groups of 20+ welcome any day except Saturday, please telephone for details.

Facilities: Kiosk, Small Shop, Tea Room.

Disabled Access: Part, please telephone for details. Toilet and parking for disabled on site.

Tours/Events: Please telephone for details.

Coach Parking: Yes

Length of Visit: 2 hours

Booking Contact: Mrs Warde/Mrs White
Squerryes Court Manor House, Westerham, Kent, TN16 1SJ
Telephone: 01959 562345 Fax: 01959 565949

Email: squerryes.court@squerryes.co.uk

Website: www.squerryes.co.uk

Location: 25 miles from London sign posted from A25. Half a mile west of centre of Westerham, 6 miles from exit 6 or 5 on the M25.

Please quote this guide when booking

Described in the Daily Telegraph as 'among the most inspirational garden acres anywhere, for everyone', the gardens are rapidly gaining a reputation for being amongst the very best in the South East. Nestling against a traditional backdrop of hop gardens and oast houses, the gardens trace garden history through sixteen landscaped displays, including a 13th century apothecary's garden, a Tudor knot, a cottager's garden in the early 19th century and a stunning herbaceous border, inspired by Gertrude Jekyll. Yalding is run by HDRA, Britain's leading organic gardening organisation, so naturally the gardens also demonstrate the best ways of making compost and how to control pests and diseases without using pesticides.

Kids will love the Children's garden. Home cooking is a speciality, using vegetables and salads fresh from the garden whenever possible - delicious! The gardens regularly appear on TV, most recently in Grassroots and the Flying Gardener.

Fact File

Opening Times: 10am - 5pm Wednesday to Sunday, May to September. Weekends only during April from Good Friday onwards and during October. Also open on Bank Holiday Mondays.

Admission Rates: Adults £3.00, Senior Citizen £3.00, Child Free

Groups Rates: Minimum group size: 14
Adults £2.50, Senior Citizen £2.50, Child Free

Facilities: Visitor Centre, Shop, Plant Sales, Teas, Restaurant.

Disabled Access: Yes. Toilet and parking for disabled on site.

Tours/Events: Monthly programme of practical demonstrations at no extra cost.

Coach Parking: Yes

Length of Visit: 2 hours

Booking Contact: Sarah Lindsay
Yalding Organic Gardens, Benover Road, Yalding, Nr Maidstone, Kent, ME18 6EX
Telephone: 02476 308211 Fax: 02476 639229

Email: enquiry@hdra.org.uk

Website: www.hdra.org.uk

Location: Half a mile south of Yalding on the B2162, 6 miles south west of Maidstone.

Please quote this guide when booking

A remarkable survival of English Garden history and the home of the Duke & Duchess of Rutland, Belvoir Castle and gardens are being sensitively restored to their former glory. The Spring Gardens contain a remarkable collection of Victorian daffodils planted sympathetically with primroses and bluebells, against a background of rhododendrons and azaleas.

Specimen trees of great rarity, many of them the largest of their type in the British Isles surround the newly restored rose garden.

Weekend events are held within the castle throughout the summer.

Fact File

Opening Times: March & October (Sundays only). 1st April - 30th September. (Closed Mondays and Fridays. Open Bank Holidays).

Admission Rates: Includes entrance into Castle - Adults £8.00, Senior Citizen £7.00, Child £5.00

Groups Rates: Minimum group size: 20
Adults £7.00, Senior Citizen £6.00, Child £4.00

Facilities: Restaurant, Gift Shop.

Disabled Access: Yes. Toilet and parking for disabled on site.

Tours/Events: Weekend events - please telephone for details.

Coach Parking: Yes

Length of Visit: 2 hours

Booking Contact: Mary McKinlay
Belvoir Castle, Belvoir, Grantham, Leicestershire, NG32 1PE
Telephone: 01476 871002   Fax: 01476 871018

Email: info@belvoircastle.com

Website: www.belvoircastle.com

Location: Close to Grantham.

Rockingham Castle stands on the edge of an escarpment giving dramatic views over five counties and the Welland Valley below.

The Castle architecture has examples from every period of its 950 year history. Surrounding the castle some 12 acres of gardens largely following the foot print of the medieval castle which houses the vast 400 year old "Elephant Hedge" that divides the formal 17th century terraced garden. The circular yew hedge stands on the site of the mot and bailey that provides a backdrop for the rose garden. Below the castle is the stunning 19th century "Wild Garden" that was replanted with advice from Kew Gardens. There are some 200 different species including a remarkable AILANTHUS altissima "Tree of Heaven" some fine SEQUOIA and a good DAVIDIA "Handkerchief Tree".

There is something to see in the garden throughout the year.

Fact File

Opening Times:	April, May and September, Sunday and Bank Holiday Monday.
	June, July and August, Sunday, Bank Holiday Monday and Tuesday from 12 noon.
Admission Rates:	Adults £7.00, Senior Citizen £6.00, Child £4.50
Groups Rates:	Minimum group size: 20
	Adults £6.00, Senior Citizen £6.00, Child £3.00
Facilities:	Shop, Restaurant.
Disabled Access:	Yes. Toilet and parking for disabled on site.
Tours/Events:	Tours of gardens with Head Gardener, Richard Stribley for booked groups of 20 or more.
Coach Parking:	Yes
Length of Visit:	2 1/2 - 3 hours
Booking Contact:	Nicola Moss
	Rockingham Castle, Rockingham, Market Harborough, Leicestershire, LE16 8TH
	Telephone: 01536 770240 Fax: 01536 771692
Email:	estateoffice@rockinghamcastle.com
Website:	www.rockinghamcastle.com
Location:	1 mile north of Corby on A6003.

Please quote this guide when booking

A traditional country house garden, with inner gardens sheltered with yew hedges. They contain a Rose Garden with a good collection of old and new roses, a White Garden, Herbaceous Borders and a Purple Border.

The central garden leads to spring and woodland gardens around a series of ponds, planted with trillium, arisaema, primulas and a multitude of spring bulbs and ferns. Beyond, a new arboretum and woodland walk.

The main Arboretum has an interesting collection of trees and shrubs and leads from the Clock House to the end of the front drive on the north side. A well designed Vegetable Garden and Orchard leads from the Main Garden through a Hornbeam tunnel with Hellebores, Hostas and Allium; Geometric border patterns for vegetables and arches of Roses and Clematis. The Orchard centre has a large Arbour planted with red vines and red climbing roses.

Fact File

Opening Times: NGS openings: Sunday 25th April - Plant Sales, Sunday 20th June - Plant Fair.
NGS days 11am - 4pm.
April to July every Tuesday 9.30am - 12.20pm.
By appointment - anytime.

Admission Rates: Adults £2.50

Facilities: Refreshments - lunch, tea etc, Plant Sales.

Disabled Access: Yes. Toilet and parking for disabled on site. Suitable for wheelchairs.

Tours/Events: None

Coach Parking: Yes

Length of Visit: 1 - 2 1/2 hours

Booking Contact: Wartnaby House, Wartnaby, Melton Mowbray, Leicestershire LE14 3HY
Telephone: 01664 822549 Fax: 01664 822231

Email: None

Website: www.wartnabyplantlabels.co.uk.com

Location: 4 miles north west of Melton Mowbray. From A606 turn left through Ab Kettleby 5 miles east of A46. Turn left at Sixhills Hotel, follow A676 towards Melton Mowbray.

Please quote this guide when booking

Newly opened to the public, 12 acres of beautiful 'lost' gardens lie in a corner of south west Lincolnshire. These important gardens have their roots in the mediaeval period, and historical connections with both plant hunters and presidents.

The Cholmeley family have lived at Easton since the 1500s, and three years ago the present Lady Cholmeley undertook a lifelong project to revive the gardens and secure their future. Formal terraces have been cleared of undergrowth, old stone walls restored and new vistas opened up. Upon this beautiful old structure a new garden for the 21st century is emerging.

Combine a visit to Easton with the opportunity to see the beautiful Castle and gardens at Grimsthorpe (see page 72). A special charge, from £10/head for groups of 20+, includes guided tours of both Easton Walled Gardens and Grimsthorpe Castle, rounded off with a cup of tea at Easton.

Fact File

Opening Times:	14th February - 22nd February 11am - 3pm.
	Wednesdays 31st March - 30th September and Bank Holiday Mondays 11am - 5pm.
Admission Rates:	Adults £3.00, Senior Citizen £3.00, Child Free
Facilities:	Plants for Sale, Teas, Gifts.
Disabled Access:	Please telephone for advice.
Tours/Events:	Pre-booked tours with owner/head gardener offered throughout the year.
Coach Parking:	Yes, pre booked only.
Length of Visit:	1 - 1 1/2 hours
Booking Contact:	The Gardens Office
	Easton Walled Gardens, Easton, Grantham, Lincolnshire, NG33 5AP
	Telephone: 01476 530063 Fax: 01476 550116
Email:	info@eastonwalledgardens.co.uk
Website:	www.eastonwalledgardens.co.uk
Location:	Just off A1, north of Colsterworth roundabout turn right along B6403
	follow signs to Easton, 1 mile on left.

Please quote this guide when booking

Discover the hidden delights of Grimsthorpe Castle Gardens. Immaculately clipped yew hedges and topiary squares sit comfortably alongside classic herbaceous borders. An unusual ornamental vegetable garden, designed in the 1960's, complements rose parterres with clipped box edges. A mini-arboretum and wild, woodland garden await discovery. Cleverly positioned vistas extend across the lake to the 17th century tree-lined avenues beyond. This is a place to relax and enjoy the tranquillity of an historic English estate. The Castle is also open and contains a collection of paintings and furniture.

Combine a visit to Grimsthorpe with an opportunity to see the rejuvenation of Easton Walled Gardens (see page 71). A special charge, from £10/head, for groups of 20+ includes guided tours of Grimsthorpe Castle and Easton Walled Gardens, rounded off with a cup of tea at Easton. Uncover the delights this part of Hidden England has to share with you.

Fact File

Opening Times:	April - September, Sunday, Thursday & Bank Holiday Mondays. (Groups anytime by appointment). Also Sunday to Thursday during August 11am - 6pm.
Admission Rates:	Adults £3.00, Senior Citizen £2.50, Child £2.00 (gardens only).
Groups Rates:	Minimum group size: 20 Adults £5.50, Child £3.00 (includes private tour of castle).
Facilities:	Tea Room, Shop, Information Room, Red Deer Herd, Woodland Adventure Playground.
Disabled Access:	Yes. Toilet and parking for disabled on site. Wheelchairs on loan, booking necessary.
Tours/Events:	Ranger guided tour of 3000 acre park in your coach. Garden tours with the Head Gardener. Special early evening private visits with candlelight supper.
Coach Parking:	Yes **Length of Visit:** 2 hours minimum
Booking Contact:	Ray Biggs Grimsthorpe Castle, The Estate Office, Grimsthorpe, Bourne, Lincs, PE10 0LY Telephone: 01778 591205 Fax: 01778 591259
Email:	ray@grimsthorpe.co.uk
Website:	www.grimsthorpe.co.uk
Location:	Situated on A151, 10 minutes drive from the A1, nearest town Bourne (3 miles).

Please quote this guide when booking

Set in 300 acres of parkland and pleasure grounds, the Victorian walled garden is a unique experience. The garden has been carefully restored to its late Victorian heyday and grows fruit, flowers and vegetables dating from 1901 or earlier. Trained fruit, vegetable beds and cut flower borders are complemented by a range of glasshouses including a peach case, vinery, display house and fernery. The huge herbaceous borders in the Secret Garden boast a colourful selection of unusual plants, whilst the Sunken Garden near the Hall is planted in pastel shades. There is also a parterre and rose beds. A 400ft long bog garden has been created in the base of the old ha-ha and a Victorian woodland garden is under development.

Fact File

Opening Times:	Park open all year, 9am - dusk. Walled Garden open 10.30am - 5pm in summer, 10.30am - 4pm in winter.
Admission Rates:	2003 prices - Adults £4.00, Senior Citizen £3.00, Child £3.00
Groups Rates:	Max group size: 30 2003 prices - Weekdays tours £30.00, Weekend and evening tours £50.00
Facilities:	Visitor Centre, Shop, Tea Room, Restaurant, Plant Sales. Regency Hall & Farm Museum also open 1pm - 4.30pm daily, during the season.
Disabled Access:	Yes. Toilet and parking for disabled on site. Wheelchairs on loan, booking necessary.
Tours/Events:	Guided tours of Walled Garden & Hall available - approx 1 1/2 hours.
Coach Parking:	Yes
Length of Visit:	3 - 4 hours
Booking Contact:	Mrs Sue Hoy Normanby Hall Country Park, Normanby, Scunthorpe, North Lincs, DN15 9HU Telephone: 01724 720588 Fax: 01724 721248
Email:	sue.hoy@northlincs.gov.uk
Website:	www.northlincs.gov.uk/normanby
Location:	4 miles north of Scunthorpe off the B1430.

Please quote this guide when booking

The Museum of Garden History is situated in a restored church building, next door to Lambeth Palace, on the banks of the River Thames. A reproduction 17th century knot garden has been created on the site of the graveyard where the tomb of 17th century plant hunters, the John Tradescants, father and son, can be seen, next to the tomb of William Bligh of the 'Bounty'.

The garden was designed by the Marchioness of Salisbury in 1981, and is based on a traditional, geometric design. It is filled with plants that were grown in Britain during the 17th century, including roses, bulbs, perennials, biennials and annuals. Surrounding the knot garden are ornamental borders also planted to the same period theme. These incorporate some fine trees such as medlar, mulberry, strawberry tree and false acacia. Topiarised myrtle, rosemary, holly and bay can also be seen.

The Museum houses a permanent collection of historic garden tools, artefacts and curiosities.

Fact File

Opening Times:	Every day - 10.30am to 5pm. Closed mid-December to early February.
Admission Rates:	Suggested donation Adults £3.00, Concessions £2.50
Facilities:	Shop, Plant Sales, Teas/Light Refreshments, Garden.
Disabled Access:	Yes but restricted
Tours/Events:	Guided tours can be booked. Seasonal Exhibitions.
Coach Parking:	No
Length of Visit:	2 hours
Booking Contact:	Susannah Williams Museum of Garden History, Lambeth Palace Road, London, SE1 7LB Telephone: 020 7401 8865 / ext 21 Fax: 020 7401 8869
Email:	info@museumgardenhistory.org
Website:	www.museumgardenhistory.org
Location:	Next door to Lambeth Palace, London SE1.

Please quote this guide when booking

A Gift For Life

How many times around Christmas and birthdays have you said, *'I have no idea what to get them as a present?'* I know I have on numerous occasions. Well, here is an idea that might help you the next time you are on the look out for that elusive present. Give a tree!

Now before you get too many images of 200 feet tall giant redwoods or mighty ancient oaks crowding into your mind, let me explain. Firstly I'm talking about saplings not mature trees and secondly I'm talking about trees which are ideal for small or medium-sized gardens and will not out-grow their surroundings.

Over the last few years there has been a large increase in the number of trees which have been purchased from garden centres and nurseries by people wanting to give them as special gifts.

So what makes a tree such a good gift? Well, firstly the choice is almost endless. There is exactly the right tree for every garden in Britain no matter how big or small. Secondly trees are living - they live alongside the person they have been given to and provide a constant reminder of the person who made the gift. They mark the passing of time through the changes of the seasons. They help bring beauty and wildlife into a garden, and on a global scale every tree helps cleanse our planet of pollutants and creates oxygen in the process. Indeed trees are essential to all life. Without trees and other plants there could be no life on earth.

But surely trees are expensive to buy I hear you say. Well, not really. The best trees to give are small young trees i.e. trees less than one metre in height. Small trees establish themselves much more readily than taller, older 'standard' trees. Depending on species, the average cost for a small tree should be less than £20.

Here are some examples of where a tree can make the ideal gift. For the birth or christening of a child. Parents can watch the tree grow alongside their baby. Choose a tree which is at its best - perhaps flowering - around the child's birthday. For anniversaries such as silver or golden. There are many trees with silver or white bark and many with golden leaves. I recently gave a maple called 'ruby glow', which had beautiful burgundy colour leaves, to a couple celebrating their 40th (ruby) wedding anniversary. Trees make ideal house warming presents and of course a wonderful commemoration for the passing of someone special. Again choose a tree which flowers or fruits around the date you wish to be remembered.

Trees will live on long after we have gone, providing a lasting living legacy - they really are a gift for life.

Tony Russell

If you would like to receive a copy of the booklet
'CHOOSING AND PLANTING THE RIGHT TREE FOR YOU'
Send a cheque of £5.00 along with your address to:

Tony Russell Associates, PO Box 32, Tetbury, Gloucestershire GL8 8BF

Capel Manor Gardens   Middlesex

Capel Manor Gardens and estate provide a colourful and scented oasis surrounding a Georgian Manor House and Victorian stables. It offers a unique opportunity to see behind the scenes at Greater London's only specialist College of Horticulture, Floristry, Garden Design, Equine, Animal Care and Countryside Studies. The attractions include, 30 acres of richly planted theme gardens including Historical Gardens, Italianate Maze, Japanese Garden. Gardening Which? Magazine demonstration and theme gardens. The National Gardening Centre with specially designed gardens. The Hessayon Centre (our Visitors Centre) with garden gift shop and floristry training shop. Selection of refreshments in our new Terrace Restaurant serving an exciting range of hot and cold food. Two unique gardens were opened at Capel in 2001 - The Diana Princess of Wales garden sponsored by pbi and Centenary garden for HM Queen Elizabeth the Queen Mother supported by the Gardens Royal Benevolent Society now known as Pelennial. Both gardens feature favourite plants for these special royal ladies.

Fact File

Opening Times:	10am - 6pm (last entry 4.30pm). Open daily March - October. Please telephone to check times.
Admission Rates:	Adults £5.00, Senior Citizen £4.00, Child £2.00
Groups Rates:	Minimum group size: 20 Adults £4.50, Senior Citizen £3.50, Child £1.50
Facilities:	Visitor Centre, Shop, Plant Sales, Restaurant, Dogs allowed entry on lead.
Disabled Access:	Yes. Parking for disabled on site. Wheelchairs on loan, booking necessary.
Tours/Events:	Please telephone for details of tours and events programme.
Coach Parking:	Yes
Length of Visit:	2 - 3 hours
Booking Contact:	Julie Ryan Capel Manor Gardens, Bullsmoor Lane, Enfield, Middx, EN1 4RQ Telephone: 0208 366 4442 Fax: 01992 717544
Email:	julie.ryan@capel.ac.uk
Website:	www.capel.ac.uk
Location:	Near junction 25 of M25.

Please quote this guide when booking

The Birmingham Botanical Gardens & Glasshouses   W Midlands

Opened in 1832, the Gardens are a 15 acre 'Oasis of Delight' with over 200 trees and the finest collection of plants in the Midlands. The Tropical House, full of rainforest vegetation, includes many economic plants and a 24ft lily pond. Palms, tree ferns and orchids are displayed in the Subtropical House. The Mediterranean House features citrus fruits and conservatory plants while the Arid House conveys a desert scene. There is colourful bedding on the Terrace plus Rhododendron, Rose, Rock, Herb and Cottage Gardens, Trials Ground and Historic Gardens. The Gardens are notably home to the National Bonsai Collection.

Other attractions include a Children's Playground, Children's Discovery Garden, exotic birds in indoor and outdoor aviaries, an art gallery and Sculpture Trail. Bands play on summer Sunday afternoons and Bank Holidays.

Fact File

Opening Times:	Open daily from 9am (10am Sundays) until dusk (7pm latest).
Admission Rates:	Adults £5.70, Senior Citizen £3.30, Child £3.30
Groups Rates:	Minimum group size: 10
	Adults £4.70, Senior Citizen £3.00, Child £3.00
Facilities:	Shop, Tea Room, Plant Sales, Children's Discovery Garden, Sculpture Trail, Aviaries, Organic Garden.
Disabled Access:	Yes. Toilet and parking for disabled on site. Wheelchairs on loan, booking necessary.
Tours/Events:	Tours by appointment. Please telephone for details of Special Events programme.
Coach Parking:	Yes by appointment.
Length of Visit:	2 - 4 hours
Booking Contact:	Tony Cartwright
	The Birmingham Botanical Gardens, Westbourne Road, Edgbaston, Birmingham, B15 3TR
	Telephone: 0121 454 1860 Fax: 0121 454 7835
Email:	admin@birminghambotanicalgardens.org.uk
Website:	www.birminghambotanicalgardens.org.uk
Location: tourist	Access from M5 junction 3 and M6 junction 6. Follow signs for Edgbaston then brown signs to Botanical Gardens.

Please quote this guide when booking

A large rose garden covering nearly two acres (0.8 Ha) and containing over 700 different varieties, considered by many to be one of the best rose gardens in the world. The garden is divided into five different areas each with their own style and mix of roses. There is a particularly good collection of Old Roses and Climbers and Ramblers in the Long Garden and Wild Roses and their near hybrids in the Species Garden. David Austin Roses are, of course, home to the English Roses and so are planted exclusively in the Renaissance Garden as well as scattered around the other areas of the garden. Other plants that associate well with roses are also found - clematis climbing up roses in the Long Garden and hardy perennials with roses in the mixed borders of the Lion Garden; this garden also contains Hybrid Teas, Floribundas and English Roses planted in formal beds. There is something of interest twelve months of the year with flowers of the early Species in March through to the last flowers of the season on the repeat flowering roses braving the elements in November and December.

Fact File

Opening Times:	9am - 5pm (7 days a week).
	9.30am - 4.30pm (Tea Shop and Restaurant).
Admission Rates:	Free entry
Groups Rates:	Free entry
Facilities:	Shop, Plant Sales, Teas, Restaurant.
Disabled Access:	Yes. Parking for disabled on site.
Tours/Events:	Workshops with the RHS.
Coach Parking:	Yes
Length of Visit:	2 - 3 hours
Booking Contact:	Jane Williams
	David Austin Roses, Bowling Green Lane, Albrighton, Wolverhampton, WV7 3HB
	Telephone: 01902 376376 Fax: 01902 372142
Email:	plant_centre@davidaustinroses.co.uk
Website:	www.davidaustinroses.com
Location:	Albrighton is situated between the A41 and A464 about 8 miles west of Wolverhampton and 2 miles south east of junction 3 on the M54. Look for the brown signs.

Please quote this guide when booking

The Bressingham Gardens Norfolk

Bressingham features not only two unique gardens: Alan Bloom's Dell Garden and Adrian Bloom's Foggy Bottom Garden, but three other developing gardens, too. The Dell Garden is renowned for its collection of 5,000 species and varieties of hardy perennials, set in six acres of park-like meadow. This delightful rural setting has colour and interest from spring to autumn and Alan Bloom's 47 Island Beds show off his wide and varied plant collection, including many Bressingham raised varieties. Foggy Bottom was created by Adrian Bloom as a garden for all seasons. Six acres of trees, conifers and shrubs provide a continuous backdrop of shape and seasonal foliage for plantings of perennials and ornamental grasses and broad grass pathways. Other newer features include The Summer Garden, with plantings of Crocosmia and the National Collection of Miscanthus, the Fragrant Garden and Adrian's Wood, which links both gardens. Blooms of Bressingham garden centre and Bressingham Steam Experience also on the same site.

Fact File

Opening Times:	April - end of October, The Dell: daily 10.30am - 5.30pm (4.30pm in October). Foggy Bottom: daily 12.30pm - 4.30pm.
Admission Rates:	(2003 prices) Adults £6.50, Senior Citizen £5.50, Child £4.00
Groups Rates:	Please telephone for group rates.
Facilities:	Visitor Centre, Shop, Tea Room, Restaurant, Kiosk, Plant Sales.
Disabled Access:	Yes. Toilet and parking for disabled on site. Wheelchairs on loan, booking necessary.
Tours/Events:	Tours available for both gardens - please book (small extra charge). Please call for details of special events.
Coach Parking:	Yes
Length of Visit:	2 - 3 hours, for plant lovers, all day.
Booking Contact:	Sue Warwick Visitor Centre, Bressingham, Diss, Norfolk, IP22 2AB Telephone: 01379 686900 Fax: 01379 688085
Email:	info@bressingham.co.uk
Website:	www.bressinghamgardens.com
Location:	Situated on A1066, two and a half miles from Diss, twelve miles from Thetford.

Please quote this guide when booking

Fairhaven Woodland and Water Garden is a haven of peace and tranquillity in the heart of the Norfolk Broads.

180 acres environmentally managed for the thriving and varied wildlife. Delightful in Spring: primroses, daffodils, skunk cabbage (Lysichitum Americanum), bluebells, followed by a spectacular display of the largest naturalised collection of Candelabra primulas in England, and azaleas and rhododendrons. An oasis in Summer, with boat trips on our private broad, flowering shrubs and wild flowers which attract several species of butterflies. Glorious Autumn colours and quietly beautiful in Winter with wonderful reflections in the still water.

A full programme of special events is available including our Green/Environmental. Please ring for details or visit our website.

Fact File

Opening Times: Open daily 10am - 5pm (closed Chrismas Day) also open until 9pm on Wednesday and Thursday evenings from May to the end of August.

Admission Rates: Adults £4.00, Senior Citizen £3.50, Child £1.50
Annual Membership: Family £35.00, Single £15.00, Wildlife Sanctuary £11.50

Groups Rates: Minimum group size: 15
Adults £3.75, Senior Citizen £3.25, Child £1.25

Facilities: Visitor Centre, Gift Shop, Tea Room, Plant Sales.

Disabled Access: Yes. Toilet and parking for disabled on site. Wheelchairs on loan, booking necessary.

Tours/Events: Guided walks or introductory talk for pre-booked groups. Programme of Special Events available, including guided walks, Music in the Garden, Green/Environmental Festival and Halloween Event.

Coach Parking: Yes   **Length of Visit:** 2 - 3 hours or preferably all day

Booking Contact: Mrs Beryl Debbage
Fairhaven Woodland & Water Garden, School Road, South Walsham, Norwich, NR13 6DZ
Telephone/Fax: 01603 270449   **Email:** fairhavengardens@norfolkbroads.com

Website: www.norfolkbroads.com/fairhaven

Location: 9 miles east of Norwich, off B1140. Signposted on A47 at junction with B1140.

Please quote this guide when booking

The Alnwick Garden   Northumberland

Set within a secretive walled garden, the first stage of this incredible garden is complete, with even more exciting plans taking shape. Its centrepiece, the Grand Cascade, is the largest water feature of its kind in the country. 7,260 gallons of water per minute tumble down the series of 30 weirs and more than 120 separate water jets are used to create a selection of different water displays. Beyond The Grand Cascade lies The Ornamental Garden, a symmetrical structured garden with a strong European influence, brimming with more than 15,000 plants. There are 'secret' gardens with places to sit and catch the sun. To the right of The Grand Cascade is The Rose Garden, a mix of pergola lined paths and grassy walkways covered in climbing and shrub roses mixed with glorious clematis and honeysuckle - the scent is heavenly. From young to old, The Garden gives pleasure to all those who visit it. It's open every day of the year, except Christmas day. This is only just the beginning. New themed gardens, a tree house and visitor centre are all planned for the future.

Fact File

Opening Times: 10am until dusk, every day except Christmas Day.

Admission Rates: Adults £4.00, Senior Citizen £3.50, Children under 16 free when accompanied by an adult

Groups Rates: Minimum group size: 14
Adults £3.50, Children under 16 free when accompanied by an adult

Facilities: Tea Room.

Disabled Access: Yes. Toilet and parking for disabled on site.

Tours/Events: Please telephone 01665 511350 for details of tours and special events.

Coach Parking: Yes

Length of Visit: At least 1 hour

Booking Contact: The Alnwick Garden, Alnwick, Northumberland, NE66 1YU
Telephone: 01665 511350 Fax: 01665 511351

Email: info@alnwickgarden.com

Website: www.alnwickgarden.com

Location: Leave the A1 North of the town at the junction signposted by the tourist information sign for The Alnwick Garden. The Garden is clearly signposted, approximately 1 mile from the A1 junction.

Please quote this guide when booking

Cragside has one of the finest high Victorian gardens in the country open to visitors. The rock garden is one of the largest in Europe and is probably the last surviving example of its type.

A fine collection of conifers, mainly from North America, is to be found in the Pinetum, below Cragside House, and across the valley lie the three terraces of the Formal Garden. On the top terrace is the Orchard House, the only remaining glass house in the gardens, which was built for the culture of early fruit. Nearby are the stone-framed carpet beds, planted for the summer season and on the middle terrace just below is the Dahlia Walk. Restoration is still in progress on the bottom, or Italian, Terrace, which contains a wonderful loggia and an imposing quatre-foil pool. Finally, the Valley garden itself is yet to be developed, but provides a wonderful setting for a gentle stroll.

Fact File

Opening Times: 30th March - 31st October, Tuesday - Sunday (and Bank Holiday Mondays).
Estate & Gardens: 10.30am - 7pm (last admission 5pm).
House: 30th March - 26th September 1pm - 5.30pm (last admission 4.30pm),
28th September - 31st October 1pm - 4.30pm (last admission 3.30pm).

Admission Rates: House, Estate & Gardens - Adults £8.00, Child (5-17) £4.00, Family £20.00.
Estate & Gardens - Adults £5.50 , Child (5-17) £2.50, Family £13.50.

Groups Rates: Minimum group size: 15: House, Estate and Gardens £6.50, Estate and Gardens £4.50.

Facilities: Visitor Centre, Shop, Restaurant.

Disabled Access: Limited. Toilet & limited parking for disabled on site. Wheelchairs on loan, booking necessary.

Tours/Events: Tours by private arrangement subject to availability. Please telephone for events programme.

Coach Parking: Yes   **Length of Visit:** Minimum 3 hours

Booking Contact: Val Miller. Cragside, Rothbury, Morpeth, Northumberland, NE65 7PX
Telephone: 01669 622001 Fax: 01669 620066

Email: val.miller@nationaltrust.org.uk

Website: www.nationaltrust.org.uk

Location: Entrance 1 mile north of Rothbury on B6341. 15 miles north west of Morpeth.
13 miles south west of Alnwick.

Please quote this guide when booking

Cotswold Wildlife Park & Gardens   Oxfordshire

Following extensive developments the Park has become an unexpected attraction to gardeners. Always a family favourite with animal lovers, garden lovers are surprised at the rich diversity of plants and planting styles encountered throughout the 160 acres of landscaped parkland surrounding a listed Victorian Manor House. Victorians would have been familiar with formal parterres and traditional herbaceous borders but not the exuberant and stunning summer displays of hardy and tender exotics including huge bananas and flamboyant cannas now found in the Walled Garden. The unique arid-scape of cactus and succulents surrounding the meerkats, the calls of Kookaburras, lemurs and macaws give this area a truly tropical ambience. The flower meadows of snowdrops, narcissus and bluebells, so welcome in the spring, contrast with the large sweeping groups of ornamental grasses and perennials which provide a wonderful foil for rhino and zebras and the many different types of bamboo which feature strongly in other animal enclosures.

Fact File

Opening Times:	Everyday (except Christmas Day). 10am. (last admission 4.30pm March - September, 3.30pm October - February).
Admission Rates:	Adults £8.00, Senior Citizen £5.50, Child £5.50 (3 - 16yrs)
Groups Rates:	Minimum group size: 20 Adults £6.50, Senior Citizen £4.50, Child £4.00
Facilities:	Shop, Teas, Restaurant. (Restaurant available for booked lunches and teas, waitress service in Orangery).
Disabled Access:	Yes. Toilet and parking for disabled on site. Wheelchairs on loan, booking necessary.
Tours/Events:	Gardens Special for inclusive charge, talk by Head Gardener or his Deputy in the Drawing Room of the Manor House and Cotswold Cream Tea in the Orangery.
Coach Parking:	Yes
Length of Visit:	2 1/2 - 3 plus hours
Booking Contact:	Lin Edgar. Cotswold Wildlife Park, Burford, Oxfordshire, OX18 4JW Telephone: 01993 823006 Fax: 01993 823807
Email:	None
Website:	www.cotswoldwildlifepark.co.uk
Location:	On A361 2.5 miles south of A40 at Burford.

Please quote this guide when booking

Visit the fabulous Waterperry Gardens and discover ornamental trees, orchards, formal gardens, meadow pastures, hidden statues and the beautiful Mary Rose Garden, not forgetting our famous 200ft south facing herbaceous border.

Enjoy unique Arts & Crafts in our resident Art in Action Gallery then visit the Country Life Museum featuring interesting agricultural implements and aspects of local history. In the garden shop choose from a range of garden equipment, seeds and bulbs, country wear, locally grown fruits, books and an attractive range of gifts and mementos. New and experienced gardeners will marvel at the large choice of top quality, Waterperry cultivated plants available in our Plant Centre. Finally enjoy some well earned refreshments in the licensed Pear Tree Tea Rooms where you can choose from a delicious selection of lunches, home made cakes, pastries and beverages many utilising fruits, herbs and produce from our own orchards and garden.

Fact File

Opening Times:	April - October - 9am - 5.30pm, November - March 9am - 5pm.
Admission Rates:	Adults £3.85, Senior Citizen £3.35, Child £2.35 under 10 Free
Groups Rates:	Minimum group size: 20
	Adults £3.10, Senior Citizen £3.10, Child £2.35 under 10 Free
Facilities:	Garden Shop, Plant Sales, Teas, Restaurant, Art in Action Gallery, Museum.
Disabled Access:	Yes. Toilet and parking for disabled on site. Wheelchairs on loan.
Tours/Events:	Tours can be arranged.
	Shakespeare 2nd July, Snowdrop weekend 14/15th February, Apple Weekend October.
Coach Parking:	Yes
Length of Visit:	Approx 3 - 4 hours
Booking Contact:	Main Office
	Waterperry Gardens, Nr Wheatley, Oxon, OX33 1JZ
	Telephone: 01844 339254 Fax: 01844 339883
Email:	office@waterperrygardens.fsnet.co.uk
Website:	www.waterperrygardens.co.uk
Location:	7 miles east of Oxford - junction 8 M40 from London. Follow brown signs.
	Junction 8a from Birmingham.

Please quote this guide when booking

The Barnsdale Garden familiar to millions of BBC2 viewers as the home of Geoff Hamilton and Gardeners' World comprises of 37 individual gardens and features that all blend together by the linking borders into one 8 acre garden.

There is not only a wealth of different plants to come and see, in many different combinations, but also an enormous amount of practical ideas for any gardener. On average most people spend about 3 hours in the garden before venturing over to the nursery where we sell a wide range of choice and unusual garden plants, many initially propagated from the gardens. So allow plenty of time to take it all in and then relax in our small and friendly licensed coffee shop which serves a very appetising range of hot and cold food and drink.

We look forward to seeing you.

Fact File

Opening Times: March - May, September & October 9am - 5pm. June - August 9am - 7pm, November - February 10am - 4pm. (Last entry 2 hours prior to closing).

Admission Rates: Adults £5.00, Senior Citizen £5.00, Child Free

Groups Rates: Minimum group size: 10
Adults £4.00, Senior Citizen £4.00, Child Free

Facilities: Shop, Tea Room, Plant Sales.

Disabled Access: Yes. Toilet and parking for disabled on site. Wheelchairs on loan, booking necessary.

Tours/Events: Yes - throughout the year.

Coach Parking: Yes

Length of Visit: 3 hours

Booking Contact: Barnsdale Gardens, The Avenue, Exton, Oakham, Rutland, LE15 8AH
Telephone: 01572 813200 Fax: 01572 813346

Email: office@barnsdalegardens.co.uk

Website: www.barnsdalegardens.co.uk

Location: A606 Oakham to Stamford and turn off at Barnsdale Lodge Hotel and we are then 1 mile on the left.

Please quote this guide when booking

Hodnet Hall Gardens   Shropshire

There has been a park and gardens at Hodnet Hall since the 11th century but their development did not begin in earnest until 1922 when pools were excavated, elders, laurels and rushes removed and a daisy chain of lakes was created. Using the natural landscape and forest trees already in place, spring bulbs, flowering shrubs and speciality trees were planted, and the season lengthened to include herbaceous borders.

So Spring arrives early in February with the first crocuses, hyacinths and early azaleas; daffodils appear in two and threes and then the carpet spreads as far as the eye can see. Bluebells shimmer in the gentle breeze of April, and Magnolia trees blossom along Magnolia Walk. May and June bring the colour and perfumes of rhododendrons and azaleas, laburnum and other many and varied flowering shrubs. July, August, and September see roses, paeonies and hydrangeas bloom and the herbaceous borders come into their own.

Fact File

Opening Times:	1st April to 30th September.
	Tuesdays to Sundays & Bank Holiday Mondays 12 noon - 5pm.
Admission Rates:	Adults £3.75, Senior Citizen £3.25, Child £1.75
Groups Rates:	Minimum group size: 25 (please pre-book) Adults £3.25
Facilities:	17th century Tea Rooms (max. seating 110), Adjacent Gift Shop,
	Kitchen Garden & Sales Area.
Disabled Access:	Yes. Toilet and parking for disabled on site. Wheelchairs on loan, booking necessary.
Tours/Events:	Guided Tours lasting 60/90 mins. Cost £22 per group. Please pre-book.
Coach Parking:	Yes
Length of Visit:	2 1/2 - 3 hours
Booking Contact:	The Secretary
	Hodnet Hall Gardens, Hodnet, Market Drayton, Shropshire, TF9 3NN
	Telephone: 01630 685786 Fax: 01630 685853
Email:	marlene@heber-percy.freeserve.co.uk
Website:	www.hodnethallgardens.co.uk
Location:	On A442 (Telford to Whitchurch) and A53 (Shrewsbury to Market Drayton).
	M6 junction 12 and 15: M54 exit 3.

One of the top ten gardens in England surrounds a magnificent 12th century home. Built of golden Hamstone it is a beautiful backdrop for a fascinating garden which has its beginnings in the early 1700's, one of the first landscaped gardens. Throughout the seasons each area has its moment of glory. The acres of Crocus, the Azaleas and Rhododendrons, the spectacular Bog garden, the colourful rock garden, and the series of cascades and ponds with the Ionic Temple serenely overlooking the herbaceous borders.

The walled kitchen garden supplies the restaurant and house with fresh vegetables and salads, and the year finishes with the beautiful autumn colours in the arboretum.

Forde Abbey is a remarkable place, with it combination of grandeur and simplicity, the quality of timelessness and of total sympathy with the countryside around, making it a unique garden with something of interest to everyone.

Fact File

Opening Times:	Gardens open daily throughout the year from 10am (last admission 4.30pm). House open April to October, 12noon - 4pm on Tue - Fri, Sundays & Bank Holiday Mondays.
Admission Rates:	Adults £5.25, Senior Citizen £4.75, Child Free
Groups Rates:	Minimum group size: 20 Adults £4.10, Senior Citizen £4.10
Facilities:	Visitor Centre, Shop, Plant Sales, Teas, Restaurant.
Disabled Access:	Yes. Toilet and parking for disabled on site. Wheelchairs on loan, booking necessary.
Tours/Events:	None.
Coach Parking:	Yes
Length of Visit:	2 hours
Booking Contact:	Mrs Carolyn Clay Forde Abbey, Chard, Somerset, TA20 4LU Telephone: 01460 220231 Fax: 01460 220296
Email:	forde.abbey@virgin.net
Website:	www.fordeabbey.co.uk
Location:	Signposted from A30 Chard to Crewkerne & from A358 Chard to Axminster. 4 miles south east of Chard.

Please quote this guide when booking

Lose yourself in 40 acres of walks, streams and temples, vivid colours, formal terraces, woodlands, lakes, cascades and views that take your breath away.

This is Hestercombe: a unique combination of three period gardens. The Georgian landscape garden was created in the 1750's by Coplestone Warre Bampfylde, whose vision was complemented with the addition of a Victorian terrace and shrubbery and the stunning Edwardian gardens designed by Sir Edwin Lutyens and Gertrude Jekyll. All once abandoned, now being faithfully restored to their former glory: each garden has its own quality of tranquility, wonder and inspiration.

Fact File

Opening Times:	Open every day 10am - 6pm (last admissions 5pm).
Admission Rates:	Adults £5.20, Senior Citizen £4.90, Child (5-15yrs) £1.30
Groups Rates:	Minimum group size: 20
	Adults £4.40
Facilities:	Visitor Centre, Shop, Plant Sales, Tea Room.
Disabled Access:	Partial. Toilet and parking for disabled on site. Wheelchairs on loan, booking not required.
Tours/Events:	Open Air Performances, Vintage Car Rallies, Hallowe'en Walks.
Coach Parking:	Yes
Length of Visit:	2 hours
Booking Contact:	Mrs Jackie Manning
	Hestercombe Gardens, Cheddon Fitzpaine, Taunton, Somerset, TA2 8LG
	Telephone: 01823 413923 Fax: 01823 413747
Email:	info@hestercombegardens.com
Website:	www.hestercombegardens.com
Location:	4 miles from Taunton,
	signposted from all main roads with the Tourist Information Daisy symbol.

Please quote this guide when booking

The garden at Milton Lodge, on the southern slope of the Mendip Hills, was conceived about 1900 by Charles Tudway, the present owner's grandfather, who transformed the sloping ground south of the house into the existing terraces, specifically to capitalise on the glorious views of Wells Cathedral and the Vale of Avalon. Rescued from the ravages of war by Mr and Mrs David Tudway Quilter, who inherited the house in 1962, the garden has since been restored to its former glory, with mixed borders, climbers, roses and yew hedges, sheltered by trees to the north and the south facing walls.

Opposite the entrance lies the Combe, a seven acre nineteenth century woodland garden, providing a peaceful oasis in pleasant contrast to the terraced garden nearby. Both share advantages of fine old trees and lovely vistas of the Cathedral and the surrounding countryside.

Fact File

Opening Times:	Tuesday, Wednesday, Sunday and Bank Holidays.
Admission Rates:	Adults £2.50, Senior Citizen £2.50, Child under 14 free
Groups Rates:	Minimum group size: 10
	Adults £3.00, Senior Citizen £3.00, Child under 14 free
Facilities:	Shop, Plant Sales, Teas on Sunday & Bank Holidays and by arrangement for groups.
Disabled Access:	Not suitable for wheelchairs.
Tours/Events:	Tours by prior arrangement only.
Coach Parking:	Minibus and SMALL coaches only on site. Others ring for details.
Length of Visit:	1 1/2 hours
Booking Contact:	Mr D Tudway Quilter
	Milton Lodge Gardens, Old Bristol Road, Wells, Somerset, BA5 3AQ
	Telephone: 01749 672168
Email:	None
Website:	None
Location:	1/2 mile north of Wells. From A39 Bristol - Wells turn north up old Bristol Road.
	Car park first gate on left.

Please quote this guide when booking

Set amongst glorious views of the Staffordshire countryside this beautiful garden, created by local landowner, Colonel Harry Clive for his wife Dorothy, embraces a variety of landscape features. They include a superb woodland garden etched from a disused gravel quarry, an alpine scree, a fine collection of specimen trees, spectacular summer flower borders and many rare and unusual plants to intrigue and delight.

A host of spring bulbs, magnificent displays of Rhododendrons and Azaleas and stunning autumn colour are among the seasonal highlights.

A fine tearoom, overlooking the garden, provides a selection of home baking and light lunches.

Fact File

Opening Times: Saturday 13th March - Sunday 31st October.

Admission Rates: Adults £3.80, Senior Citizen £3.30, Child 11-16 £1.00, up to 11 Free

Groups Rates: Minimum group size: 20
Daytime £3.30, Evening £3.80

Facilities: Tea Room.

Disabled Access: Yes. Toilet and parking for disabled on site. Wheelchairs on loan, booking necessary.

Tours/Events: None.

Coach Parking: Yes

Length of Visit: 1 1/2 hours

Booking Contact: Mrs Marianne Grime (Secretary)
The Dorothy Clive Garden, Willoughbridge, Market Drayton, Shropshire, TF9 4EU
Telephone: 01630 647237 Fax: 01630 647902

Email: None

Website: www.dorothyclivegarden.co.uk

Location: On the A51, two miles south from the village of Woore. From the M6 leave at Junction 15, take the A53, then the A51.

Please quote this guide when booking

Kew Gardens   Surrey

Kew Gardens, World Heritage Site, is paradise throughout the seasons. Lose yourself in the magnificent conservatories, and discover plants from the world's deserts, mountains and oceans. Wide-open spaces, stunning vistas, listed buildings and wildlife contribute to the Gardens' unique atmosphere.

Why not tie in your visit with one of these seasonal festivals: The Orchid festival (14 February - 14 March) with over 100,000 orchids in unforgettable displays. Spring to Life (20 Mach - 16 May) offers 3 months of flowering splendour. Go Wilder (29 May - 26 September) celebrates the beauty of Britain's biodiversity. Rich autumn colour at Autumn Cornucopia (11 October - 2 November). Christmas at Kew (December - early January) with shimmering lights and seasonal activities. There are also great places to eat and shop, a museum and interactive exhibition, unique art galleries and the Kew Explorer to transport you around the key highlights.

Fact File

Opening Times:	Open daily at 9.30am. Closing times vary through the season.
Admission Rates:	Adults £7.50, Senior Citizen £5.50, Child Free (under 16 yrs)
Groups Rates:	Minimum group size: 10 (must be pre-paid)
	Adults £6.00, Senior Citizen £4.40, Child Free
Facilities:	Visitor Centre, Shop, Plant Sales, Teas, Restaurant.
Disabled Access:	Yes. Toilet and parking for disabled on site. Wheelchairs on loan, booking necessary.
Tours/Events:	Five Seasonal Festivals per year.
	Walking tours at specific times. Daily Kew guided tours (11am & 2pm).
Coach Parking:	Yes
Length of Visit:	2 - 3 hours
Booking Contact:	Travel Trade Office
	Kew Gardens, Richmond, Surrey, TW9 3AB
	Telephone: 020 8332 5648 Fax: 020 8332 5610
Email:	info@kew.org
Website:	www.kew.org
Location:	Silverlink and District Line to Kew Gardens. South West trains to Kew Bridge Station. Buses 65 and 391. Parking on Kew Road (A307) and in Ferry Lane car park.

Please quote this guide when booking

Part of the magnificent grounds of Loseley Park, the original two and a half acre Walled Garden is largely based on a design by Gertrude Jekyll.

The Garden features five exquisite gardens, each with its own theme and character. The award-winning **Rose Garden** is planted with over one thousand old-fashioned rose bushes. The **Herb Garden** contains six separate sections devoted to culinary, medicinal, ornamental, dye plants, cosmetics and wildlife. The **Flower Garden** is designed to provide interest and colour throughout the season. The **White Garden** is serene, idyllic and tranquil with the central water feature flanked by borders of white, cream and silver plants. The **Vegetable** and **Cut Flower Garden** has an amazing variety of common and unusual plants and has stunned visitors with its displays. The **Moat**, with its associated **Moat Walk** runs almost the entire length of the Walled Garden and is abundant with wildlife and pond plants.

Fact File

Opening Times:	5th May - 30th September, Wednesday - Sunday, 11am - 5pm. May and August Bank Holidays.
Admission Rates:	Adults £3.00, Senior Citizen £2.50, Child £1.50
Groups Rates:	Minimum group size: 10 Adults £2.75, Senior Citizen £2.25, Child £1.25
Facilities:	Lunchtime Restaurant, Courtyard Teas, Shop, Plant Sales.
Disabled Access:	Yes. Toilet and parking for disabled on site. Wheelchairs on loan.
Tours/Events:	House tours and garden tours for groups by arrangement. Special evening tours with wine, music and canapes - contact for details.
Coach Parking:	Yes
Length of Visit:	2 hours
Booking Contact:	Nicky Rooney Loseley Park, Estate Office, Guildford, Surrey, GU3 1HS Telephone: 01483 405120 Fax: 01483 302036 General Information: 01483 304440
Email:	enquiries@loseley-park.com
Website:	www.loseley-park.com
Location:	3 miles south of Guildford via A3 and B3000.

Please quote this guide when booking

Savill Garden - Windsor Great Park   Surrey

World renowned 35 acre woodland garden within Windsor Great Park which was created in 1932 by Sir Eric Savill from an undeveloped area of the Park. Spectacular Spring displays; formal rose gardens and herbaceous borders in Summer; fiery colours of Autumn and misty vistas of Winter. The unique temperate house shelters frost-tender plants from the rigours of Winter - "a piece of woodland under glass".

In celebration of the Golden Jubilee, a new area has been created, designed by award winning Barbara Hunt; planting created and executed by Lyn Randall, Head of the Savill Garden, and a water sculpture by Barry Mason. The theme is soft and peaceful, a summer garden with hard landscaping.

Having walked round this delightful garden, enjoy a relaxing meal in the excellent restaurant and perhaps treat yourself to something from the plant and gift shop. An oasis of tranquillity 5 miles from Windsor.

Fact File

Opening Times: 10am - 6pm March - October, 10am - 4pm November - February.

Admission Rates: Seasonal - Adults £3.50 - £5.50, Senior Citizen £3.00 - £5.00, Child £1.25 - £2.50

Groups Rates: Minimum group size: 10
Seasonal - Adults £3.00 - £5.00, Senior Citizen £3.00 - £5.00, Child £1.25 - £2.50

Facilities: Shop, Plant Sales, Teas, Restaurant.

Disabled Access: Yes. Toilet and parking for disabled on site. Wheelchairs on loan.

Tours/Events: Guided tours for groups, bookable in advance.
On-going programme of events - please contact for details.

Coach Parking: Yes

Length of Visit: 3 - 4 hours

Booking Contact: Julie Hill
Crown Estate Office, The Great Park, Windsor, Berkshire, SL4 2HT
Telephone: 01753 847518 Fax: 01753 847536

Email: savillgarden@crownestate.co.uk

Website: www.savillgarden.co.uk

Location: Clearly signposted from Ascot, Bagshot, Egham, Windsor, Old Windsor and A30.

Please quote this guide when booking

Titsey Place

Surrey

Titsey is one of the largest surviving historic estates in Surrey. It dates back to the mid-sixteenth century, through the first impression now is of a comfortable early - nineteenth century house in a picturesque park, under the North Downs which hereabouts rise to over 800 feet.

It is difficult to believe that this well-preserved stretch of country is barely twenty miles from the centre of London; only the M25 motorway intrudes into a landscape which otherwise has hardly changed in the last hundred years. The estate was originally bought in 1534 by Sir John Gresham, of the famous London Merchant dynasty, and descended in the early-nineteenth century through the female line to the Leveson Gowers, a cadet branch of the family of the Dukes of Sutherland. The Leveson Gower family lived at Titsey till the death of Thomas Leveson Gower in 1992.

Fact File

Opening Times:	Mid May - end of September, Wednesdays and Sundays 1pm - 5pm. Also May and August Bank Holidays and then garden only Easter Monday.
Admission Rates:	Adults £5.00, Senior Citizen £5.00, Garden only £2.50
Groups Rates:	Please telephone for details.
Facilities:	Picnic Area, use of Botley Hill Farmhouse at top of Titsey Hill offering lunches by arrangement.
Disabled Access:	Limited wheelchair access.
Tours/Events:	Guided tours of house and garden by arrangement. Occasional special events.
Coach Parking:	Yes by arrangement
Length of Visit:	2 - 3 hours
Booking Contact:	Kate Moisson. c/o Strutt and Parker, 201 High Street, Lewes, BN7 2NR Telephone: 01273 407056 Fax: 01273 478995
Email:	kate.moisson@struttandparker.co.uk
Website:	www.titsey.com
Location:	From the A25, between Oxted and Westerham, turn left onto B629 at the end of Limpsfield High Street turn left and follow Blue signs to visitors car park.

Please quote this guide when booking

A woodland garden on the grand scale; set beneath the canopies of beautiful mature trees with delightful views to Virginia Water Lake. Over 200 acres of camellias, rhododendrons, magnolias and many other flowering trees and shrubs provide visitors with a breathtaking display in March, April and May.

Massed plantings of hydrangeas are the highlight of the summer before a myriad of autumn tints from Japanese maples, birches, sweet gums and tupelos light up the woods.

Winter brings the flowers of witch-hazels and drifts of heathers amongst the dwarf conifers in the Heather Garden before swathes of dwarf daffodils stud the turf in the sweeping Azalea Valley.

Truly a garden for all seasons.

Fact File

Opening Times:	Car park open: 8am - 7pm (4pm in winter) or sunset if earlier.
Admission Rates:	Car Park Charges only: April & May £5.50, June - March £4.00
Facilities:	At nearby Savill Garden.
Disabled Access:	Yes but limited. Toilet and parking for disabled on site.
Tours/Events:	None
Coach Parking:	No. Coaches by arrangement only on weekdays.
Length of Visit:	2 - 3 hours
Booking Contact:	Julie Hill
	Valley Gardens - The Great Park, Windsor, Berkshire, SL4 2HT
	Telephone: 01753 847518 Fax: 01753 847536
Email:	savillgarden@crownestate.co.uk
Website:	None
Location:	On the eastern boundary of Windsor Great Park (off A30).
	Access to Valley Gardens car park via Wick Road.

RHS Garden Wisley   Surrey

A garden to enjoy whatever the time of year. RHS Garden Wisley, demonstrates British gardening at its best with 240 acres of glorious garden. There is a greater horticultural diversity found at Wisley than any other garden in the world, providing visitors with ideas and inspiration for every kind of garden. From the beginning of the year colour is every where with pastels of the blossom and delicate spring bulbs in early spring to the bright colours of the camellias and rhododendrons in late spring. During summer the garden explodes with colour from the traditional Mixed Borders and Rose gardens to the modern Grass Borders and perennial planting of the Piet Oudolf borders. Yellows, oranges and reds of the shrubs and trees dominate autumn in the Arboretum, Pinetum, and Wild Garden, whilst winter is quiet and peaceful with the shapes and structures showing through. Lastly not forgetting the Fruit Field, Vegetable Garden, Glasshouses and Rock Garden.

Fact File

Opening Times:	All year except Christmas Day. Monday - Friday 10am - 6pm (4.30pm November - February) Saturday and June 9am - 6pm (4.30pm November - February).
Admission Rates:	Adults £7.00, Senior Citizen £7.00, Child £2.00
Groups Rates:	Minimum group size: 10 Adults £5.50, Senior Citizen £5.50, Child £1.60
Facilities:	Café, Restaurant, Coffee Shop, Plant Centre, Gift Shop.
Disabled Access:	Yes. Toilet and parking for disabled on site. Wheelchairs on loan, booking necessary.
Tours/Events:	Many special events throughout the year, please telephone for details.
Coach Parking:	Yes
Length of Visit:	4 hours
Booking Contact:	Sarah Martin RHS Garden Wisley, Woking, Surrey, GU23 6QB Telephone: 01483 212307 Fax: 01483 211750
Email:	sarahm@rhs.org.uk
Website:	www.rhs.org.uk
Location:	In Surrey, near to junction 10 of the M25 on the A3.

Please quote this guide when booking

Gardens & Grounds of Herstmonceux Castle — East Sussex

Herstmonceux is renowned for its magnificent moated castle, set in beautiful parkland and superb Elizabethan gardens. Built originally as a country home in the mid 15th century, Herstmonceux Castle embodies the history of medieval England and the romance of renaissance Europe. Set among carefully maintained Elizabethan gardens and parkland, your experience begins with your first sight of the castle as it breaks into view.

In the grounds you will find the formal gardens including a walled garden dating from before 1570, a herb garden, the Shakespeare Garden, woodland sculptures, the Pyramid, the water lily filled moat and the Georgian style folly.

The woodland walks will take you to the remains of the three hundred year old sweet chestnut avenue, the rhododendron garden from the Lowther/Latham period, the waterfall (dependent on rainfall), and the 39 steps leading you through a woodland glade.

Fact File

Opening Times: 9th April - 24th October, open daily.

Admission Rates: Adults £4.50, Senior Citizen £3.50, Child £3.00 (5-15yrs)

Groups Rates: Minimum group size: 15
Adults £3.50, Senior Citizen £3.00, Child/Students £2.00 (5-15yrs)

Facilities: Visitor Centre, Shop, Plant Sales, Tea Room, Nature Trail, Children's Woodland Play Area.

Disabled Access: Limited. Toilet and parking for disabled on site. 1 wheelchair on loan, booking essential.

Tours/Events: Tours Sunday - Friday (subject to availability) extra charge.
11th April Easter Egg Hunt challenge.

Coach Parking: Yes

Length of Visit: 2 - 4 hours

Booking Contact: Caroline Dennett
Herstmonceux Castle, Hailsham, East Sussex, BN27 1RN
Telephone: 01323 834457 Fax: 01323 834499

Email: c_dennett@isc-queensu.ac.uk

Website: www.herstmonceux-castle.com

Location: Located just outside the village of Herstmonceux on the A271, entrance is on Wartling Road.

Please quote this guide when booking

Boasting England's longest water-filled medieval moat encircling seven acres of beautiful grounds and gardens, discover 800 years of history at Michelham Priory.

On this peaceful "island of history" explore the impressive 14th century gatehouse, working watermill and magnificent (reputedly haunted) Tudor mansion that evolved from the former Augustinian Priory. In the grounds ingenious planting of the landscaped gardens offers the visitor an ever-changing display of beauty, whatever the season, while the physic and cloister gardens add extra interest.

Fact File

Opening Times: 1st March - 31st October, Tuesday - Sunday from 10.30am.
Also open daily in August and on Bank Holiday Mondays.
Closing times, March and October 4pm, April - July and September 5pm, August 5.30pm.

Admission Rates: Adults £5.20, Senior Citizen £4.50, Child £2.70

Groups Rates: Minimum group size: 15. Adults £4.25, Senior Citizen £4.25, Child £2.45
Free admission for coach drivers and tourist guides on production of a 'blue badge'.

Facilities: Shop, Restaurant, Café, Plant Sales.

Disabled Access: Yes. Toilet and parking for disabled on site. Wheelchairs on loan, booking advised.

Tours/Events: Guided tours organised for groups as requested. Easter Garden Festival 10 - 12 April.

Coach Parking: Yes. Free refreshments for coach drivers.

Length of Visit: 3 - 4 hours

Booking Contact: Henry Warner. Michelham Priory, Upper Dicker, Nr Hailsham, East Sussex, BN27 3QS
Telephone: 01323 844224 Fax: 01323 844030

Email: adminmich@sussexpast.co.uk

Website: www.sussexpast.co.uk

Location: 2 miles west of Hailsham & 8 miles north west of Eastbourne. Sign-posted from A22 & A27. (OS map 198 TQ558 093).

Please quote this guide when booking

The de Passele family built a moated Manor in 1262 and held the estate until 1453, when it was sold to the forebears of Anne Boleyn. It is possible that Anne, second wife of Henry VIII, stayed here during her childhood. In 1543 the estate was sold to Sir Thomas May, who built the Tudor house you see today, the fine Georgian façade was added in 1720.

The Gardens offer a sumptuous blend of romantic landscaping, imaginative plantings and fine old trees, fountains, springs and large ponds. This is a quintessentially English Garden of a very individual character, with exceptional views to the surrounding valleyed fields. Many eras of English history are reflected here, typifying the tradition of the English Country House and its Garden.

Pashley now holds a Tulip Festival in May, Spring and Summer Plant Fairs, The Summer Flower Festival, The Sussex Guild Craft Show and an exhibition of Sculptures lasting throughout the season.

Fact File

Opening Times:	6th April - End September, Tuesday, Wednesday, Thursday & Saturday 11am - 5pm.
Admission Rates:	Adults £6.00, Senior Citizen £5.50, Child £5.50 (0 - 6 years Free)
Groups Rates:	Minimum group size: 20
	Adults £5.50, Senior Citizen £5.50
Facilities:	Shop, Plant Sales, Teas, Licensed Café, Light Lunches.
Disabled Access:	Limited. Toilet and parking for disabled on site. Wheelchairs on loan, booking necessary.
Tours/Events:	Tours of garden available. Please call for special event details.
Coach Parking:	Yes
Length of Visit:	2 1/2 hours
Booking Contact:	Claire Baker
	Pashley Manor Gardens, Ticehurst, East Sussex, TN5 7HE
	Telephone: 01580 200888 Fax: 01580 200102
Email:	info@pashleymanorgardens.com
Website:	www.pashleymanorgardens.com
Location:	On the B2099 between the A21 and Ticehurst village (Tourist brown-signed).

Please quote this guide when booking

In Spring, the sumptuous blooms of **azaleas and rhododendrons** (some 200 years old) overhang paths **lined with bluebells** in this romantic 240-acre valley with walks around **seven lakes**.

Watch the wallabies, wildfowl and deer. Enjoy the glorious **Rock Garden**, admire the art of beautiful **Bonsai**, and marvel at the collection of **Victorian Motorcars** (1889-1900).

Visit the extended **"Behind the Doll's house"** exhibition. This shows a country estate and local hamlet of 100 years ago - all in miniature 1/12th scale.

The **Clock Tower Restaurant** for morning coffee, lunches and teas. There is a **Gift Shop** and a wide selection of **Plants for sale**.

Fact File

Opening Times: 1st April - 31st October 9.30am - 6pm.

Admission Rates: May (Saturdays, Sundays & Bank Holiday Mondays) £8.00, May (Monday - Friday) £7.00, April & June to October £6.00, Children - anytime (5 - 15 yrs) £4.00

Groups Rates: Minimum group size: 20
May (Saturdays, Sundays & Bank Holiday Mondays £7.00, May (Monday - Friday) £6.00
April & June to October £5.00, Children - anytime (5 - 15yrs) £3.50

Facilities: Shop, Restaurant, Plant Sales.

Disabled Access: No

Tours/Events: 1-2-3 May Bonsai Weekend & demonstration, 26 & 27 June West Sussex Country Craft Fair, 17 & 18 July Model Boat Regatta & Veteran Car rally

Coach Parking: Yes (Free) **Length of Visit:** 4 - 5 hours

Booking Contact: Robin Loder. Leonardslee Gardens, Lower Beeding, Horsham, West Sussex, RH13 6PP
Telephone: 01403 891212 Fax: 01403 891305

Email: gardens@leonardslee.com

Website: www.leonardslee.com

Location: 4 miles from Handcross at bottom of M23 via B2110, entrance is at junction of B2110 and A281, between Handcross and Cowfold.

Please quote this guide when booking

Mature trees and shrubs planted within the 7.5 acre woodland garden of the late horticulturalist Arthur Hellyer and his wife Gay is now enhanced with naturalistic herbaceous planting of immense beauty. Many of Hellyer's books were inspired by the making of this garden. Daffodils, snowdrops, aconites, hellebores *Pulmonaria* and *Scilla messeniaca* herald the spring, through summer exuberance to glorious autumn colour. Every shade of green can be seen in the tree canopies, country garden planting in the borders, hardly a scrap of bare earth!

Nature joins in this eclectic mix, *Claytonia sibirica* groundcover beneath the trees, seeding itself on the roof of an old shed. Bluebells naturalize amongst the rhododendrons and camellias, stitchwort and cow parsley light up dull corners. Spotted orchids follow on from the cowslips in the meadows. Feel the peace; listen to the birdsong in this tranquil setting.

Fact File

Opening Times:	3rd March - 30th October, Wednesday, Thursday, Friday & Saturday.
Admission Rates:	Adults £3.00, Senior Citizen £2.50, Child Free if accompanied
Groups Rates:	Guided Tours - pre booked £6.00 per person
Facilities:	Plant Sales, Teas (self-service but not a machine), B/B x 1 twin en suite, pre-booked.
Disabled Access:	No.
Tours/Events:	Guided (pre booked) groups only £6.00 per person.
Coach Parking:	No
Length of Visit:	1 1/2 hours minimum
Booking Contact:	Penelope Hellyer (Mrs)
	Orchards, off Wallage Lane, Rowfant, Nr Crawley, West Sussex, RH10 4NJ
	Telephone: 01342 718280
Email:	penelope.hellyer@hellyers.co.uk
Website:	www.hellyers.co.uk
Location:	Equidistant Crawley Down and Turners Hill villages. Wallage Lane off B2028 immediately after railway bridge turn right into Farm Lane.

Please quote this guide when booking

Wakehurst Place Gardens   West Sussex

Wakehurst Place was leased by the Royal Botanic Gardens, Kew, in 1965 from the National Trust. Situated in an 'Area of Outstanding Natural Beauty' on the High Weald of Sussex. Its range of microclimates complement the conditions at Kew and allow the plant collection to be enhanced. Collections of temperate trees and shrubs were established by Gerald Loder (1st Lord Wakehurst) between 1903 and 1936 and added to by Sir Henry Price to 1963.

Kew has since developed the collections and arranged them into geographic areas, suggesting a walk through the temperate woodlands of the world. Features include a Himalayan Glade, water gardens and cottage-style plantings in the walled gardens. A large part is designated as a Site of Special Scientific Interest by English Nature. The Loder Valley Nature Reserve, on the southern flank of the estate, gives visitors the opportunity to observe wildlife at close quarters and provides a refuge for the flora and fauna of the Sussex Weald.

Fact File

Opening Times:	10am daily - 4pm November, December & January, February 5pm, March 6pm, April - September 7pm, October 6pm.
Admission Rates:	Adults £7.00, Senior Citizen £5.00, Child 16 years and under Free
Groups Rates:	Minimum group size: 10 Prices on application.
Facilities:	Visitor Centre, Shop, Plant Sales, Restaurant, Exhibition in Millennium Seed Bank. (Shop and Restaurant close 1 hour before grounds).
Disabled Access:	Yes. Toilet and parking for disabled on site. Wheelchairs on loan.
Tours/Events:	Tours available. Occasional special events and exhibitions.
Coach Parking:	Yes
Length of Visit:	3 - 4 hours
Booking Contact:	Administration Wakehurst Place, Ardingly, Haywards Heath, West Sussex, RH17 6TN Telephone: 01444 894066 Fax: 01444 894069
Email:	None
Website:	None
Location:	From London M23 junction 10. B2028 - 7 miles north of Haywards Heath.

Please quote this guide when booking

West Dean Gardens   West Sussex

Visiting West Dean Gardens, winner of the Historic Houses Association/Christie's Garden of the Year 2002, you are immersed in a classic 19th Century designed landscape.

Its 2 1/2 acre highly acclaimed restored Victorian walled kitchen and fruit gardens, 13 original glasshouses dating from the 1890's, 35 acres of ornamental grounds, 240 acre landscaped park and the 49 acre St Roche's arboretum are all linked by a scenic 2 1/4 mile parkland walk. Features of the grounds include a 300 ft long Edwardian pergola designed by Harold Peto hosting numerous climbers. Restoration of late Regency flint and rock work around the river, rebuilding of the 1820's summer house and replacement of a lost Laburnum arch combined with a contemporary planting scheme make this an exciting addition to the already expansive grounds.

The Visitor Centre houses a quality licensed restaurant and an imaginative garden shop.

Fact File

Opening Times: Open daily March - October. March, April & October 11am - 5pm.
May - September 10.30am - 5pm.
Admission Rates: Adults £5.50, Senior Citizen £5.00, Child £2.00
Groups Rates: Minimum group size: 20
Adults £5.00, Senior Citizen £5.00, Child £2.00
Facilities: Visitor Centre, Shop, Plant Sales, Teas, Restaurant.
Disabled Access: Limited. Toilet and parking for disabled on site. Wheelchairs on loan, booking necessary.
Tours/Events: Tours by appointment only.
Annual events programme, please enquire for details.
Coach Parking: Yes
Length of Visit: 2 - 4 hours
Booking Contact: Celia Dickinson
West Dean Gardens, West Dean, Chichester, West Sussex, PO18 0QZ
Telephone: 01243 818221   Fax: 01243 811342
Email: gardens@westdean.org.uk
Website: www.westdean.org.uk
Location: On A286 6 miles north of Chichester.

Please quote this guide when booking

Only twelve years ago the grounds were mainly grass and orchards - but today visitors can discover several different gardens including an Elizabethan knot garden, a rose labyrinth, a superb walled garden and extensive herbaceous borders, amongst others.

The showpiece of the whole garden is the 1.5 acre walled garden. This exciting project was opened in 1996 and has since matured into a splendid series of individual 'garden rooms'. The rose labyrinth is a particularly stunning feature, and during the summer months it becomes rich with colour and perfume. Also in the walled garden there are beautiful herbaceous borders whilst plants nurtured at Coughton Court are on sale to visitors.

Thanks to the enthusiasm of the Throckmorton family, the gardens are taking shape as some of the finest in the country. In fact, the gardens have now become as big a draw as the house itself.

Fact File

Opening Times:	Check visitor information line on 01789 762435.
Admission Rates:	House & Gardens: Adults £8.25, Child (under 16) £4.15 under 5's Free
	Gardens only: Adults £5.50, Child £2.75
Groups Rates:	Minimum group size: 15
	House & Gardens: £7.00, Gardens only: £4.65
Facilities:	Shop, Plant Sales, Teas, Restaurant, Gunpowder Plot Exhibition.
Disabled Access:	Yes to gardens only. Toilet and parking for disabled on site.
	Wheelchairs on loan, booking necessary.
Tours/Events:	There is a programme of events and gardening activity from March to Christmas.
Coach Parking:	Yes
Length of Visit:	2 hours
Booking Contact:	Coughton Court, Alcester, Warwickshire, B49 5JA
	Telephone: 01789 400777 Fax: 01789 765544
Email:	sales@throckmortons.co.uk
Website:	www.coughtoncourt.co.uk
Location:	Take the A435 from Alcester towards Birmingham, the House is signposted from this road.

Please quote this guide when booking

Ryton Organic Gardens   Warwickshire

The UK's premier centre for organic gardening, now with - The Vegetable Kingdom - a new £2million fully interactive visitor centre telling the story of Britain's vegetables and the importance of preserving rare varieties.

Outside there are over five acres of gardens, including stunning flower borders, herbs, shrubs, a delightful children's garden and, of course, lots of interesting and unusual vegetable and fruit - some grown in window boxes, through to entrancing potagers.

Also, learn the best ways of making compost and how to control pests, diseases and weeds without using chemicals.

Enjoy a delicious home cooked meal in our restaurant, or relax with an organic cappuccino in the orangery coffee shop. A greatly enlarged new shop provides lots to tempt you! The gardens regularly appear on television, including BBC Gardener's World'.

Fact File

Opening Times: 9am - 5pm.
Admission Rates: Adults £3.95, Senior Citizen £3.95, Child £1.50
Facilities: Visitor Centre, Shop, Plant Sales, Teas, Restaurant.
Disabled Access: Yes. Toilet and parking for disabled on site. Wheelchairs on loan, booking necessary.
Tours/Events: Regular programme of events at no extra cost.
Coach Parking: Yes
Length of Visit: Half a day
Booking Contact: Sarah Lindsay
Ryton Organic Gardens, Coventry, CV8 3LG
Telephone: 02476 308211 Fax: 02476 639229
Email: enquiry@hdra.org.uk
Website: www.hdra.org.uk
Location: Off the A45 on the road to Wolston 5 miles south east of Coventry.

Please quote this guide when booking

A funny thing happened on the way to the Phormium at Abbey House Gardens, Malmesbury, home to Ian & Barbara Pollard

Imagine the scene. Ian crumpled over a raised bed in the herb garden rooting out wild euphorbia which had dared to grow under a lavender bush. Suddenly the hair on the back of his legs signals the approach of a visitor. Since BBC Gardener's World broadcast a half hour special on our gardens in June 2002, it has been increasingly difficult to finish a task without interruption and Ian wonders which plant he'll be asked to identify of the 10,000 we've planted. As he twists to stand, the visitors hands come into view and stacked in her grip are about 30 of our plant labels. Ian's temperature begins to rise and it's nothing to do with the sun. The hands extend themselves towards him proffering the labels and a voice full of amusement explains;

"My children have been having such fun collecting these. They competed to see who collected most, but I expect it's easiest for you to put them back because you'll know where they go".

She is gone before Ian can speak, which is just as well as anything he said would not have been polite. Our challenge to design and plant the neglected 5 acres we bought in 1994 has been achieved without a master plan being drawn up. We planned to do this later having carefully labelled everything first. Fine plan!!

Since the broadcast though the most common comment made to me as I de-head our 2000 different roses or crouch to weed the herbaceous borders is:-

"Aah there you are....I didn't recognise you with your clothes on!!"

The Gardener's World team filmed for a day every other month over a year to capture the change of Seasons with us. Naturally we got to know the crew quite well and towards the end of filming offered them supper during which Ian let slip that he gardens in the nude. We discussed many topics but for some reason, this was the fact written up for a synopsis of the programme! A lovely photographer was sent to take photographs to accompany the article and we subtly "Adam & Eve'd it" for the Radio Times. Little did I expect to then see our full frontles exposed in both the Daily Mail and the News of the World!!

'The WOW! factor is here in abundance' Alan Titchmarsh. 5 acre gardens of fantastic colour throughout the season. Lovely camellias set off a fabulous display of over 50,000 bulbs including an amazing display of tulips. A superb collection of iris's follows in May with wisteria, laburnum and a growing collection of rhododendrons and azaleas. Throughout summer 2,000 different roses in bloom are a breathtaking sight continuing until the frosts, supported by lilies and alstoemeria. The beautiful double herbaceous borders have been compared to Monet's and the wooded river walk creates contrast in scale, atmosphere and planting. A unique herb garden, a foliage garden, hydrangeas, many specimen trees and shrubs take you through to autumn colour and all against the dramatic back drop of Malmesbury Abbey. The ancient hill top town itself with shops, cafes and museum adds even more for a wonderful day out.

Fact File

Opening Times: 11am - 6pm 21st March - 21st October (11am - 5.30pm from 2005).
Admission Rates: Adults £5.00, Senior Citizen £4.75, Child £2.00
Groups Rates: Minimum group size: 20
Adults £4.50, Senior Citizen £4.50, Child £2.00
Facilities: Plant Sales, Teas.
Disabled Access: Yes.
Tours/Events: Sculpture Exhibitions and plays.
Coach Parking: No
Length of Visit: 2 hours minimum
Booking Contact: Aly Sunderland
Abbey House Gardens, Market Cross, Malmesbury, Wiltshire, SN16 9AS
Telephone: 01666 827650 Fax: 01666 822782
Email: info@abbeyhousegardens.co.uk
Website: www.abbeyhousegardens.co.uk
Location: Head for Malmesbury town centre off A429 between M4 Junction 17 (5 miles) and Cirencester. Follow signs to long stay (free) car park. Walk across Mill Lane bridge, climb Abbey steps and enter gardens left of Cloister Garden.

Please quote this guide when booking

The Bowood Rhododendron Gardens cover some sixty acres, surrounding Robert Adam's magnificent Mausoleum.   The first Rhododendrons were introduced by the 3rd Marquis of Lansdowne in 1850. His Grandson, on retiring as Viceroy in 1894, created the main structure of the woodland walks, planting mainly hardy hybrids, many of which are unavailable today. Over the past forty years, the present Lord Lansdowne, and his Father before him, have added many hundreds of new varieties. A collection of broad-leafed plants came from the island of Ghia; another group of plants grown from seed collected by Roy Lancaster at 11,000 feet from Yunan in 1981. Planting and thinning continues season after season. This garden is where man and nature are in harmony. An hour or more strolling along the network of paths looking over a sea of bluebells, with magnolias and giant Loderii reaching for the light between the overhanging oak canopy, is where paradise can be found.

Fact File

Opening Times: House & Gardens: 1st April - 31st October.
Rhododendron Walks: 6 week flowering season, late April to early June.

Admission Rates: Adults £6.40, Senior Citizen £5.30, Child £4.10 (5-15yrs) £3.25 (2-4yrs)
Just Rhododendrons £3.60

Groups Rates: Minimum group size: 20 (N/A for just Rhododendron Walks)
Adults £5.45, Senior Citizen £4.65, Child £3.60 (5-15yrs) £3.05 (2-4yrs)

Facilities: At House & Garden: Visitor Centre, Shop, Teas, Restaurant, Adventure Playground, Coffee Shop.

Disabled Access: Partial. Toilet and parking for disabled on site. Wheelchairs on loan, booking necessary.

Tours/Events: Pre-booked guided tours available. For 2004 Special Events please visit the web site.

Coach Parking: Yes.   **Length of Visit:** 3 plus hours House & Gardens. 2 plus hours Rhododendron Walks.

Booking Contact: Mrs Jane Meadows. Bowood House, The Estate Office, Derry Hill, Calne, Wilts,SN11 0LZ.
Telephone: 01249 812102   Fax: 01249 821757

Email: houseandgardens@bowood.org

Website: www.bowood.org

Location: House & Gardens: Off A4 midway between Chippenham and Calne.
Rhododendron Walks: Off A342 between Chippenham and Devizes.

Please quote this guide when booking

Heale House Garden & Plant Centre

Heale House and its eight acres of beautiful garden, lie beside the river Avon, at Middle Woodford, just north of Salisbury. Much of the house is unchanged since King Charles II hid here in 1651.

In January great drifts of snowdrops and aconites bring early colour and this promise of spring is followed by magnificent magnolias and acers that surround the authentic Japanese Tea House and red Niko Bridge. The garden provides wonderfully varied collection of plants, shrubs, musk and other roses, a working kitchen garden, all growing in the formal setting of clipped hedges and mellow stonework and particularly lovely in June and July. As Summer turns to Autumn, Cyclamen, Nerines and Viburnums are in flower and trees and shrubs in the Japanese Garden display their brilliant autumnal foliage before leaf fall and the start of winter flowering shrubs and Hellebores.

Fact File

Opening Times:	Garden: Tuesday - Sunday 10am - 5pm (open Bank Holiday Mondays) all year.
	Plant Centre: Monday - Sunday 10am - 5pm all year.
Admission Rates:	Adults £3.75, Senior Citizen £3.75, Child £1.50 (5-15yrs)
Groups Rates:	Minimum group size: 20
	Adults £3.50, Senior Citizen £3.50, Child £1.50 (5-15yrs)
Facilities:	Shop, Plant Sales, Light Refreshments only.
Disabled Access:	Yes.
Tours/Events:	Snowdrop weekends' 1st and 8th February. Guided tour and hot food on these first Sunday's in February of the Snowdrop and winter Aconite display.
Coach Parking:	Yes
Length of Visit:	1 1/2 - 2 hours
Booking Contact:	Mr Andrew Flitcroft. Heal House, Middle Woodford, Nr Salisbury, Wiltshire, SP4 6NT
	Telephone: 01722 782504 Fax: 01722 782504
Email:	None
Website:	None
Location:	Four miles from Salisbury, Wilton and Stonehenge, on the 'Woodford Valley' road between the A360 and A345.

Please quote this guide when booking

The splendour of Longleat House nestling alongside a lake and within rolling 'Capability' Brown landscaped grounds is a view that cannot be missed. Fringed by thousands of trees the grounds include formal gardens, a 'Secret Garden' the 'Pleasure Walk', a 19th century planting of rhododendrons and azaleas, topiary and fine examples of mazes including the Love Labyrinth, the Sun Maze and the Lunar Labyrinth.

A recent addition to Longleat are standing stones at Heaven's Gate - the massive stones and a ring-shaped 'gateway' - made up of 13 smaller stones - from part of a gigantic sculpture which was commissioned by the Seventh Marquess of Bath.

Fact File

Opening Times:	27th March to 31st October 2004.
Admission Rates:	Adults £16.00, Senior Citizen £13.00, Child £13.00 (3-14yrs)
Groups Rates:	Minimum group size: 12
	Adults £12.00, Senior Citizen £9.75, Child £.9.75 (3-14yrs)
Facilities:	Shops, Restaurant, Café.
Disabled Access:	Yes. Toilet and parking for disabled on site. Wheelchairs on loan, booking necessary.
Tours/Events:	See website www.longleat.co.uk
Coach Parking:	Yes
Length of Visit:	A full day
Booking Contact:	Scott Sims
	Longleat, Warminster, Wiltshire, BA12 7NW
	Telephone: 01985 844328 Fax: 01985 844763
Email:	enquiries@longleat.co.uk
Website:	www.longleat.co.uk
Location:	Longleat is situated just off the A36 between Bath and Salisbury (A362 Warminster - Frome).

Please quote this guide when booking

The Peto Garden Wiltshire

Romantically sited overlooking the valley of the River Frome, close to Bradford-on-Avon, Iford Manor is built into the hillside below a hanging beechwood and fine garden terraces. The house was owned during the first part of the last century by Harold Peto, the architect and landscape designer who taught Lutyens, and who expressed his passion for classical Italian architecture and landscaping in an English setting. After many visits to Italy he acquired statues and architectural marbles. He planted phillyrea and cypress trees and other Mediterranean species to add to the plantings of the eighteenth century and to enhance the Italian character of the garden. The great terrace is bounded on one side by an elegant colonnade and commands lovely views out over the orchard and the surrounding countryside.   Paths wander through the woodland and garden to the summerhouse, the cloister and the casita and amongst the water features.

Fact File

Opening Times:	2pm - 5pm Sundays April and October.
	2pm - 5pm Tuesday - Thursday May to September.
	Mondays and Fridays reserved for group visits by appointment.
Admission Rates:	Adults £4.00, Senior Citizen £3.50, Child over 10 yrs £3.50
Groups Rates:	Minimum group size: 8
	Adults £4.50, Senior Citizen £4.50, Child over 10 yrs £4.50
Facilities:	House Keeper Teas - May to August at weekends.
Disabled Access:	Yes. Toilet and parking for disabled on site.
Tours/Events:	By appointment.
Coach Parking:	Yes
Length of Visit:	1 1/2 hours
Booking Contact:	Mrs Elizabeth Cartwright-Hignett
	The Peto Garden, Iford Manor, Bradford on Avon, Wiltshire, BA15 2BA
	Telephone: 01225 863146 Fax: 01225 862364
Email:	None **Website:** www.ifordmanor.co.uk
Location:	Follow brown tourist signs to Iford Manor. 7 miles south of Bath on A36 Warminster Road and 1/2 a mile south of Bradford on Avon on B3109.

Please quote this guide when booking

Pound Hill is a 2 acre, garden planted in a romantic, English style. Its reputation for design and horticultural excellence is widely acknowledged and it was recently appointed as a partner garden to the Royal Horticultural Society.

The garden has been laid out as a series of individually designed rooms, in scale with the central 16th century Cotswold farmhouse. You approach the garden through an inspiring retail nursery, which has a most inviting selection of herbaceous, topiary and roses. Inside the garden you encounter a formal kitchen garden and a small rose garden planted with old roses. The main part of the garden is laid out with structure given by box hedging, yew cones in the design of deep 'Jekyll' borders, lawn and parterre. There is also a courtyard garden, a wildlife pond and avenues of white-stemmed birch and clipped chestnuts with inspiring underplanting.

Fact File

Opening Times:	Plant Centre daily & Bank Holidays 10am - 5pm, closed January.
	Garden daily & Bank Holidays 2pm - 5pm March - October.
Admission Rates:	Adults £3.50, Senior Citizen £3.50, Child Free
Facilities:	Shop, Plant Sales, Coffee, Lunch, Tea, Restaurant, Study Mornings, RHS Advisors.
Disabled Access:	Yes. Parking for disabled on site.
Tours/Events:	Please telephone for details of special events. RHS study mornings, expert lectures, wholesale nursery open days.
Coach Parking:	Yes
Length of Visit:	2 hours
Booking Contact:	Philip Stockitt
	Pound Hill, West Kington, Chippenham, Wiltshire, SN14 7JG
	Telephone: 01249 783880 Fax: 01249 782953
Email:	info@poundhillplants.co.uk
Website:	www.poundhillplants.co.uk
Location:	From Bath or the M4 junction 18 follow the A46 and turn onto the A420 towards Chippenham. After 2.5 miles follow brown signs to Pound Hill.

Please quote this guide when booking

An outstanding example of the English landscape style, this splendid garden was designed by Henry Hoare II and laid out between 1741 and 1780. Classical temples, including the Pantheon and the Temple of Apollo, are situated around the central lake at the end of a series of vistas, which change as the visitor moves around the paths and through the magnificent mature woodland with its extensive collection of trees and shrubs.

Although Stourhead has changed and developed over more than two centuries, it remains as Horace Walpole described it in the 18th century: "One of the most picturesque scenes in the world".

The Stourhead Estate extends from the edge of the Wiltshire Downs in the east to King Alfred's Tower in the west, a 160 ft folly with views across Somerset, Dorset and Wiltshire.

Fact File

Opening Times: All year, daily from 9am until 7pm, or dusk if earlier.
(House open Friday - Tuesday, 19th March - 31st October).

Admission Rates: Adults £5.40, Child £3.00, National Trust Members free

Groups Rates: Minimum group size: 15
Adults £4.80, National Trust Members free

Facilities: Visitor Centre, Shop, Plant Sales, Self Service Restaurant, Spread Eagle Inn.

Disabled Access: Yes. Toilet and parking for disabled on site. Wheelchairs on loan.

Tours/Events: Many different group packages available including lunch or refreshments. Please ask for the Group Information Guide. Walks, talks, painting, music, theatre & childrens events take place all year. For events leaflet call 01747 841152.

Coach Parking: Yes   **Length of Visit:**   Minimum 2 hours

Booking Contact: Gill Harris. Stourhead Estate Office, Stourton, Nr Mere, Warminster, Wiltshire, BA12 6QD
Telephone: 01747 841152   Fax: 01747 842005

Email: stourhead@nationaltrust.org.uk

Website: www.nationaltrust.org.uk/stourhead

Location: Stourhead is in the village of Stourton, off the B3092, 3 miles north west of Mere(A303).
It is 8 miles south of Frome (A361).

Please quote this guide when booking

This jewel in Worcestershire's crown was, until two years ago, opened only occasionally to the public and is possibly the oldest privately owned Arboretum in the country. It is a haven of peace and tranquillity which overlooks the banks of the River Severn close to the picturesque village of Upper Arley. Approached through rolling parkland, entrance is made through a listed Walled Garden which contains an Italianate Garden, raised beds, orchard, herbaceous borders, ornamental fowl, picnic area and plant sales.

With planting commencing in 1820 by Lord Mountnorris, it is now a mature and majestic Arboretum with awe-inspiring trees (some of which are record breaking and includes the tallest Crimean Pine in Britain) underplanted with rhododendrons, azaleas and camellias and 1000's of spring flowering bulbs together with a delightful Magnolia Walk.

Fact File

Opening Times: 1st April - 31st October.
Wednesday, Thursday, Friday, Sunday & Bank Holiday Mondays 10am - 5pm.

Admission Rates: Adults £3.00, Senior Citizen £3.00, Child £1.00

Groups Rates: Minimum group size: 20 - £2.00, under 20 - £2.50

Facilities: Picnic Area, Refreshments, Plant Sales, Dogs on leads.

Disabled Access: Yes. Toilet and parking for disabled on site. Wheelchairs on loan.

Tours/Events: None.

Coach Parking: Yes

Length of Visit: 2 hours

Booking Contact: Jenny Emms
Arley Arboretum, Arley Estate Office, Arley, Nr Bewdley, Worcs, DY12 1XG
Telephone: 01299 861368 Fax: 01299 861330

Email: info@arley-arboretum.org.uk

Website: www.arley-arboretum.org.uk

Location: Off the A442 - Kidderminster/Bridgnorth/Telford Road - brown signed from Shatterford on A442.

Please quote this guide when booking

Bodenham Arboretum

Worcestershire

Bodenham Arboretum has been awarded National Heritage status for the creation of a new English landscape and Arboretum, and a Centre of Excellence by the Forestry Authority who described it as "a showpiece woodland rich in habitats for wild flowers, water-fowl and other birds".

Over 2700 species of trees and shrubs landscaped within 156 acres, incorporating a working farm. Four miles of paths through dells, glades, lakes, pools, and fields where sheep and cattle graze, and rare breeds of poultry roam. Daffodils and primroses in March and April, bluebells in May, the laburnum tunnel from mid May to mid June and the vibrant colours in Autumn are special attractions for visitors.

The unique underground visitors centre with its restaurant overlooking the big pool, won the CLA President award for the best new rural building in England and Wales 1998/99.

Fact File

Opening Times:	Open every day, 11am - 5pm (or dusk) all year round.
Admission Rates:	Adults £4.00, Senior Citizen £4.00, Child £1.50, Wheelchair Users £1.50
Groups Rates:	Minimum group size: 25
	Adults £3.50, Senior Citizen £3.50, Child £1.50 (no charge for teachers in school parties)
Facilities:	Visitor Centre, Restaurant, Shop. January & February weekdays - no restaurant facilities.
Disabled Access:	Yes, Visitor Centre fully accesible, Arboretum limited access.
	Toilet and parking for disabled on site. Wheelchairs on loan, booking advised.
Tours/Events:	Guided tours by arrangement £25 1 - 11/2 hours.
	Plant Fair, RHS 'Walk & Talk' lectures 26th April & 11th October 2pm - 5pm.
	Please ring for details.
Coach Parking:	Yes
Length of Visit:	2 hours - all day.
Booking Contact:	James Binnian. Bodenham Arboretum, Wolverley, Kidderminster, DY11 5SY
	Telephone: 01562 852444 Fax: 01562 852777
Email:	None
Website:	www.bodenham-arboretum.co.uk
Location:	Map reference SO 8081. Brown signs from Wolverley Church Island along B4189 (2 miles).

Please quote this guide when booking

Famed for its National Collection of Clematis, Burford House Gardens holds around 500 varieties of this popular species. During the summer there may be as many as 80 in flower at one time.

Uniquely situated at the confluence of the Ledwych Brook and the River Teme the herbaceous borders of this traditional English garden overflow with colourful plantings throughout the summer and early autumn, while ferns and bamboos thrive in the streamside areas. The gardens of this elegant Georgian house also feature many specimen trees providing colour and interest through to the autumn.

The adjacent garden centre stocks over 350 varieties of clematis as well as a fine range of roses, shrubs, trees and herbaceous plants. The Café Bar offers freshly prepared food every day.

Fact File

Opening Times: Open all year Monday - Sunday 9am - 6pm. (Gardens close at dusk if earlier).
Admission Rates: Adults £3.95, Senior Citizen £3.95, Child £1.00
Groups Rates: Minimum group size: 20
Adults £3.00, Senior Citizen £3.00, Child £1.00
Facilities: Garden Centre (Free), Café Bar.
Disabled Access: Yes. Toilet and parking for disabled on site. Wheelchairs on loan, booking advised.
Tours/Events: Tours available by prior arrangement.
Coach Parking: Yes
Length of Visit: 1 - 2 hours
Booking Contact: Burford House Gardens
Burford Garden Company, Tenbury Wells, Worcestershire, WR15 8HQ
Telephone: 01584 810777   Fax: 01584 810673
Email: info@burford.co.uk
Website: www.burford.co.uk
Location: 8 miles from Ludlow on A456, 1 mile west of Tenbury Wells.

Please quote this guide when booking

Snowshill Manor Garden Worcestershire

This delightful Arts and Crafts garden was designed by its owner Charles Paget Wade, in collaboration with M. H. Baillie Scott, as a series of outdoor rooms.

The first National Trust garden to be managed following organic principles, it is a lively mix of cottage flowers, bright colours and delightful scents with stunning views across the Cotswold countryside. A tranquil spot to enjoy the sounds of running water, bird song and the wind in the trees.

The Manor, home to Wade's collection of craftsmanship and design, will be closed in 2004 for essential work.

Fact File

Opening Times: 19th March - 31st October.
11am - 5.30pm Wednesday - Sunday including Bank Holiday Mondays.

Admission Rates: Adults £3.80, Senior Citizen £3.80, Child £1.90

Facilities: Shop and Restaurant.

Disabled Access: Yes. Toilet and parking for disabled on site. Wheelchairs on loan.

Tours/Events: We have a series of events throughout the year, please telephone for details.
Guided tours are available on request.

Coach Parking: Yes by appointment only.

Length of Visit: 1 1/2 hours

Booking Contact: Property Assistant
Snowshill Manor, Snowshill, Broadway, Worcestershire, WR12 7JU
Telephone: 01386 842 814 Fax: 01386 842822

Email: snowshillmanor@nationaltrust.org.uk

Website: www.nationaltrust.org.uk

Location: 2 1/2 miles south west of Broadway; turn from A44 Broadway bypass into Broadway village and by village green turn uphill to Snowshill.

Please quote this guide when booking

This lovely 30 acre garden is owned by the Berkeley family, whose other home is historic 12th Century Berkeley Castle in Gloucestershire. At Spetchley you will find most aspects of gardening, the formal and informal, woodland and herbaceous. A Garden full of secrets, every corner reveals some new vista, some new treasure of the plant world, whether it be tree, shrub or plant. The exuberant planting and the peaceful walks make this an oasis of peace and quiet. Many of the vast collection of plants are rarely found outside the major botanical gardens. The wonderful display of spring bulbs in April and May, together with flowering trees and shrubs, are followed in June and July by the large selection of roses, whilst July, August and September reveal the great herbaceous borders in all their glory. This is indeed a garden for all seasons.

Fact File

Opening Times: 1st April - 30th September. Tuesday - Friday 11am - 6pm, Sundays 2pm - 6pm, Bank Holiday Mondays 11am - 6pm. Closed all Saturdays and all other Mondays. Last admissions on all opening days 4pm.

Admission Rates: Adults £4.00, Senior Citizen £4.00, Child £2.00

Groups Rates: Minimum group size: 25
Adults £3.80, Senior Citizen £3.80, Child £1.90

Facilities: Tea Room.

Disabled Access: Yes. Parking for disabled on site. Booking necessary for parties.

Tours/Events: Special Plant Fair 25th April 2004.

Coach Parking: Yes

Length of Visit: 2 hours minimum

Booking Contact: Mr R Berkeley
Spetchley Park, Worcester, Worcs, WR5 1RS
Telephone: 01905 345213 or 345224 Fax: 01453 511915

Email: hb@spetchleygardens.co.uk

Website: www.spetchleygardens.co.uk

Location: 2 miles east of Worcester on A44, leave M5 at either junctions 6 or 7.

Please quote this guide when booking

This enchanting garden of trees covers 127 acres and has impressive sweeping Vistas, lakes and ponds. Visit our glades of rare *Sorbus*, marvel at the unique evergreen oak, the silver foliaged coyote willow from Mexico, the pretty Cretan *Zelkova* and the very rare *Eucalyptus neglecta* from the mountains of Victoria, Australia. One of our prime objectives is the conservation of trees and shrubs, which are endangered, or have disappeared, from their natural habitats.

There is much to see and enjoy throughout the year. Watch the birdlife from the Bird Observatory, picnic beside the lake. In spring admire our displays of woodland flowers, drifts of stately blue camassias, and the plantation of stunning wild pear blossom. In summer see the elegant show of blue poppies in the rootery garden. Come again in Autumn and warm to the changing of colours as over 5,000 trees and shrubs display their autumn colours.

Fact File

Opening Times:	2nd March to 31st October, every day except Mondays. 10am - last admissions 4pm. Gates close 6pm every day Tuesday to Sunday and Bank Holidays.
Admission Rates:	Adults £3.75, Senior Citizen £3.75, Child £1.75
Groups Rates:	Minimum group size: 10
	Adults £3.25, Senior Citizen £3.25, Child £1.00
Facilities:	Nearby
Disabled Access:	Yes. Parking for disabled on site. Wheelchair on loan, booking necessary.
Tours/Events:	Tours for groups of 10 or more £5.00 per person by pre booking only.
Coach Parking:	Yes
Length of Visit:	2 hours
Booking Contact:	M Carmichael. Castle Howard Arboretum Trust, Castle Howard, York, YO60 7DA Telephone: 01653 648650
Email:	mcarmichael@castlehoward.co.uk
Website:	www.kewatch.co.uk
Location:	17 miles north east of York - off A64. Follow the brown & white tourist signs to Castle Howard and look for our entrance by the Gatehouse Archway.

Please quote this guide when booking

One of the most remarkable sites in Europe, sheltered in a secluded valley, Fountains Abbey and Studley Royal, a World Heritage Site, encompasses the spectacular remains of a 12th century Cistercian abbey with one of the finest surviving monastic watermills in Britain, an Elizabethan mansion, and one of the best surviving examples of a Georgian green water garden. Elegant ornamental lakes, avenues, temples and cascades provide a succession of unforgettable eye-catching vistas in an atmosphere of peace and tranquillity. St Mary's Church, built by William Burges in the 19th century, provides a dramatic focal point to the medieval deer park with over 500 deer.

Small museum near to the Abbey. Exhibitions in Fountains Hall, Swanley Grange and the Mill.

Fact File

Opening Times: April - September 10am - 6pm, October - March 10am - 4pm.
Closed Fridays in November - January and closed 24th and 25th December.

Admission Rates: Adults £5.50, Senior Citizen £5.50, Child £3.00, NT/EH Members Free

Groups Rates: Minimum group size: 31 plus (Also do a 15 - 30 group rate - please call for details)
Adults £4.50, Senior Citizen £4.50, Child £2.20, NT/EH Members Free

Facilities: Visitor Centre, Shop, Tea Room, Restaurant, Kiosk.

Disabled Access: Yes. Toilet and parking for disabled on site. Wheelchairs on loan, booking necessary.

Tours/Events: Guided tours for groups, must be pre booked, telephone 01765 643197.
Annual events programme, please enquire for details.

Coach Parking: Yes

Length of Visit: 1 1/2 hours mimimum

Booking Contact: Fountains Abbey, Ripon, Yorkshire, HG4 3DY
Telephone: 01765 608888   Fax: 01765 601002

Email: fountainsenquiries@nationaltrust.org.uk

Website: www.fountainsabbey.org.uk

Location: 4 miles west of Ripon off B6265 to Pateley Bridge, sign posted from A1,
10 miles north of Harrogate A61.

Please quote this guide when booking

Originally established in 1950 as a trial garden, Harlow Carr recently became the first RHS Garden in the north. A beautiful and peaceful garden stretches across 58 acres and highlights include: streamside garden with candelabra primulas; flower, fruit and vegetable trials; contemporary grass border; scented, herb and foliage gardens; woodland and arboretum to name but a few. The gardens are constantly developing, and new for 2004 are the BBC 'Gardens through Time' - seven historical gardens reflecting gardening history over the last 200 years, and marking the RHS bicentenary this year.

Masses of fascinating events take place throughout the year including outdoor theatre, festivals and children's activities. An extensive range of over 70 gardening & horticulture workshops is also available. With free parking, picnic areas, Cafe Bar, Plant Centre & Shop, Museum of Gardening, courses and full events programme, Harlow Carr is one of Yorkshire's most relaxing locations.

Fact File

Opening Times:	9.30am - 6pm (or dusk if sooner), open every day of the year.
Admission Rates:	Adults £5.00, Senior Citizen £4.50, Child £1.00 (for over 6's)
Groups Rates:	Minimum group size: 10
	£4.00 per person
Facilities:	Largest Gardening Bookshop in the north, Gift Shop, Café Bar, Plant Centre.
Disabled Access:	Yes. Toilet and parking for disabled on site. Wheelchairs on loan, booking necessary.
Tours/Events:	A full programme of events is available from the gardens. Frequent garden tours available.
Coach Parking:	Yes
Length of Visit:	1 - 2 hours
Booking Contact:	Moira Malcolm
	RHS Garden Harlow Carr, Crag Lane, Harrogate, HG3 1QB
	Telephone: 01423 565418 Fax: 01423 530663
Email:	admin-harlowcarr@rhs.org.uk
Website:	www.rhs.org.uk
Location:	Take the B6162 Otley Road out of Harrogate towards Beckwithshaw. Harlow Carr is 1.5 miles on the right.

Please quote this guide when booking

Newby Hall was built between 1691-1695, shortly afterwards the owner, Sir Edward Blackett, commissioned Peter Aram to lay out formal gardens in keeping with the period. Very little of Aram's layout for Newby remains today and the present design is largely attributable to the present owner's grandfather, the late Major Edward Compton, who inherited in 1921. Influenced by Lawrence Johnston's Hidcote Manor in Gloucestershire, he created a main axis for the garden running from the south front of the house down to the River Ure. The axis consisted of double herbaceous borders flanked by yew hedges. Either side of the borders are numerous compartmented gardens such as the Rose Garden, the Autumn Garden, the Rock Garden, the Laburnum pergola walk, a Water Garden and even a Tropical Garden here in North Yorkshire - truly a 'Garden for all Seasons'. Newby also holds the National Collection of CORNUS.

Fact File

Opening Times:	1st April - end of September, 11am - 5.30pm, Tuesday - Sunday & Bank Holidays.
Admission Rates:	(2003 Rates).
	Adults £5.70, Senior Citizen £4.70, Child £4.20
Groups Rates:	Minimum group size: 15
	Adults £4.60, Senior Citizen £4.60, Child £3.70
Facilities:	Visitor Centre, Shop, Plant Sales, Teas, Restaurant.
Disabled Access:	Yes. Toilet and parking for disabled on site. Wheelchairs on loan, booking necessary.
Tours/Events:	Tours on request with pre-booking essential.
Coach Parking:	Yes
Length of Visit:	2 hours minimum
Booking Contact:	Rosemary Triffit
	Newby Hall, Ripon, North Yorkshire, HG4 5AE
	Telephone: 01423 322583 Fax: 01423 324452
Email:	info@newbyhall.com
Website:	www.newbyhall.com
Location:	2 miles from A1M at Ripon exit - junction 48.

Please quote this guide when booking

These substantial walled gardens and wooded pleasure grounds, recently restored and much improved, are well worth visiting in all seasons: massive herbaceous borders, Victorian kitchen garden with rare vegetable collection, the National Hyacinth Collection, herb and shade borders, extensive hothouses and thousands of snowdrops, bluebells, daffodils and narcissi. A stroll around the lake takes you through the deer park, where fallow deer graze beneath the boughs of living oak trees, now believed to be over a thousand years old. This walk also offers the best views of the 14th century castle.

Guided tours of the castle give you a chance to view the civil war armour, secret priests hiding hole and splendid furnishings. On site facilities include ample free parking, wc's (including disabled), tea room, historic inn with beer garden and gift shop selling plants.

Fact File

Opening Times:	Daily - throughout the year 9am - 5pm (dusk in the winter months).
Admission Rates:	Adults £3.50, Senior Citizen £3.00, Child £2.00 (under 5 yrs Free)
Groups Rates:	Minimum group size: 15 people
	Adults £3.00, Senior Citizen £3.00, Child £2.00
Facilities:	Gift Shop, Plant Sales, Tea Rooms, Restaurant.
Disabled Access:	Yes. Toilet and parking for disabled on site. Wheelchairs on loan, booking necessary.
Tours/Events:	Guided tours of gardens by prior arrangement only.
Coach Parking:	Yes
Booking Contact:	Mrs Wendy McNae
	Ripley Castle Gardens, Ripley, Nr Harrogate, North Yorkshire, HG3 3AY
	Telephone: 01423 770152 Fax: 01423 771745
Email:	groups@ripleycastle.co.uk
Website:	www.ripleycastle.co.uk
Location:	Three miles north of Harrogate on the A61.

Please quote this guide when booking

Jersey

Set in a tranquil valley and accessed only by a small country lane, Judith and Nigel Quérée have created a garden with a diverse collection of 1,700 mainly herbaceous perennials from all over the world. Full of interesting features such as a bog garden viewed from an elevated wooden walkway and the attractive old granite cottage that is built into the side of the valley.

For that personal touch walk with Judith around the garden to see the many rare and unusual plants in this eclectic collection, plants such as Arisaemas, Clematis, Irises and Salvias. There is a wide variety of habitat in this relatively small garden from hot and dry for the sun loving plants through to damp and shady where the Chinese and American woodlanders thrive.

There is plenty to interest the keen gardener who is looking for a garden with a difference.

Fact File

Opening Times:	Tuesday, Wednesday and Thursday - 1st May to 30th September.
Admission Rates:	Adults £4.00, Senior Citizen £4.00, Child £2.00
Facilities:	Small range of unusual plants for sale, Picnic Area available.
Disabled Access:	No.
Tours/Events:	By guided tour only with Judith - 11am and 2pm. By appointment only.
Coach Parking:	No, other arrangements can be made, please telephone for details.
Length of Visit:	Up to 2 hours
Booking Contact:	Judith Quérée
	Creux Baillot Cottage, Le Chemin Des Garennes, St Ouen, Jersey, Channel Islands, JE3 2FE
	Telephone: 01534 482191 Fax: 01534 482191
Email:	judith@judithqueree.com
Website:	www.judithqueree.com
Location:	Map can be sent prior to visit or directions given by telephone.

Please quote this guide when booking

Lost Garden Of International Importance
Re-Discovered' On Jersey

It was once described as, 'the most diverse garden in the British Isles', 'a subtropical paradise', 'a species of fairy land'.

Walking through what remains of the eight acre Samuel Curtis garden of La Chaire at Rozel Bay, Jersey today, it is difficult to attribute these descriptions to it. The only clues to this once great garden are crumbling wall and steps, old lead irrigation pipes, weed-covered terracing and giant, ancient trees; their broken branches and dead limbs telling the story of the last hundred years.

In 1900 this was a garden like no other, a subtropical garden of such diversity that it was the principal attraction of Jersey, one that every tourist to the island expected to visit.

It was the creation of the great Victorian plantsman Samuel Curtis, who had spent years scouring the British Isles for a location where he could grow outside many of the subtropical plants being grown under glass at Kew. In 1841 he found it, a sheltered, hidden valley, facing the sea at Rozel Bay, Jersey.

With the help of W.J.Hooker, Director of the Royal Botanic Gardens at Kew, Curtis began to amass and plant tender exotics from all over the world. By the time of his death in 1860 he had established one of the most unique gardens in Britain and in the process pushed the boundaries of what could be grown outside further than anyone before, or possibly since.

For 50 years after his death the garden thrived and then a succession of owners and a World War began the almost inevitable decline. This was hastened during the Second World War when occupying German forces dug up some of what was left of the Curtis plant collection and transported them back to Germany.

From then until 2002 much of the garden became neglected, its former glory and importance understood by just a handful of Jersey residents. The only garden maintenance was concentrated around a hotel called Chateau la Chaire, which sits at the entrance to the garden.

Then in the spring of 2002, Angie Petkovic, owner of APT Marketing Solutions, a PR and marketing company based in Cheltenham, stumbled across the garden. "It was one of those moments that you never forget. Although I enjoy gardening I know very little about gardens and yet I just felt this garden must have been special".

She asked BBC gardening writer, broadcaster and former Head Forester of Westonbirt Arboretum, Tony Russell to come and take a look. "The second I got there I realised that this had been a garden of some significance. The extensive terracing complete with south facing beds, the careful use of topography and aspect throughout the garden, and the smattering of unusual and exotic plants, such as a magnificent 100 year-old Canary Island Date Palm, all suggested the work of a skilled and knowledgeable horticulturist".

Over the following months the story of the Samuel Curtis garden at La Chaire began to be pieced together. By the end of 2002 both Angie Petkovic and Tony Russell were convinced that such an important garden should, if at all possible, be restored faithfully to the original Samuel Curtis concept.

During 2003 a historical survey and restoration plan of the whole site was carried out and funds are now being actively sought for the gardens restoration.

In the meantime there is an opportunity for gardening and horticultural groups to visit and enjoy the magical experience of walking through a garden which has been lost in time for almost 100 years. A chance to see what it looks like before the restoration work begins and to hear first hand of the plans for restoration.

If you would like to visit the Sub-tropical gardens of La Chaire please contact Angie Petkovic on:
telephone number 01242 250692.

Scotland

*"The quality of light surpasses all other places ... as the
mist lessens the loch glistens whilst the gorse and heather
burst into flame. Even the funereal peat softens,
as if in response to the deepening red of the pine."*

'On the Western Isle' E.B. Hamilton

Scottish gardens are unique. They may contain
(in some instances) similar plants and architecture to their
English cousins but there the similarity ends. The rich acid soils,
abundance of water and clarity of air combine to create plants
of great vigour and stunning vistas - both within the garden
and to the borrowed landscape beyond. From Castle Kennedy
in the south to Dunvegan Castle on the Isle of Skye this book
provides a choice selection of Scotland's finest gardens.

Opposite: Drummond Castle Gardens (page 133)

Armadale Castle Gardens & Museum of the Isles has a spectacular setting within the Sleat Peninsula of the Isle of Skye called the 'Garden of Skye'.

The forty acre Garden is set around the ruins of Armadale Castle. The warm, generally frost free climate of the west coast of Scotland - a result of the Gulf Stream - allows these sheltered gardens, dating back to the 17th Century, to flourish.

Wander over the expanses of lawn leading from the ruined Armadale Castle to viewpoints overlooking the hills of Knoydart. Terraced walks and landscaped ponds contrasting with wildflower meadows bring the natural and formal side by side. The Nature Trails provide another dimension to this garden experience. In May during the bluebell season, a carpet of blue around the Arboretum creates a visual and fragrance sensation that is so prevalent around the gardens at that time of year.

Fact File

Opening Times:	9.30am to 5.30pm (last entry 5pm), 7 days April to October (incl).
Admission Rates:	Adults £4.60, Senior Citizen £3.20, Child £3.20
Groups Rates:	Minimum group size: 8
	Adults £2.90, Senior Citizen £2.90, Child £2.90
Facilities:	Visitor Centre, Shop, Garden Shop, Restaurant, Museum of the Isles, Gift Shops.
Disabled Access:	Yes. Toilet and parking for disabled on site. Electric wheelchairs on loan, booking necessary.
Tours/Events:	Guided walks available on request. Garden & Craft Fair - last weekend in May.
Coach Parking:	Yes
Length of Visit:	2 hours
Booking Contact:	Mags MacDonald
	Armadale Castle, Armadale, Sleat, Isle of Skye, IV45 8RS
	Telephone: 01471 844305 Fax: 01471 844275
Email:	office@clandonald.com
Website:	www.clandonald.com
Location:	2 minutes from Armadale/Mallaig Ferry. 20 miles from Skyebridge on A851.

Please quote this guide when booking

Hercules Garden is a walled garden of ten acres, over looked by a fine statue of Hercules by John Cheere, placed on a rise in a shrub walk running east from Blair Castle, the ancestral home of the Dukes of Atholl. It was the 2nd Duke who landscaped the grounds in the mid 18th century, his scheme evolved to create two ponds in a large walled garden designed in the 'Ferme Ornee' manner-fruit and vegetables grown among ornamental planting schemes and sweet smelling shrubs.

Today the garden contains a large collection of fruit trees, a terrace over 300 meters long flanked by herbaceous borders, a variety of beds for vegetables, herbs, cut flowers, shade loving plants, roses and annuals. The layout is based on the 2nd Duke's design and includes some of the original statuary, a recreation of the Chinese bridge, heather thatched huts for the nesting birds and a restored folly, housing a display about the restoration of the garden.

Fact File

Opening Times:	9.30am - 4.30pm last entry.
Admission Rates:	Grounds & Garden: Adults £2.00, Senior Citizen £2.00, Child £1.00
Groups Rates:	As above.
Facilities:	Shop, Teas, Restaurant, Castle (5 star historic home).
Disabled Access:	Yes. Toilet and parking for disabled on site. Wheelchairs on loan, booking necessary.
Tours/Events:	Please call for details or visit website.
Coach Parking:	Yes
Length of Visit:	approx 2 hours
Booking Contact:	Admin Office
	Blair Castle, Blair Atholl, Pitlochry, Perthshire, PH18 5TL
	Telephone: 01796 481207 Fax: 01796 481487
Email:	office@blair-castle.co.uk
Website:	www.blair-castle.co.uk
Location:	Off A9 at Blair Atholl on Perth / Inverness Road (35 mins Perth).
	1 1/2 hours Edinburgh.

Please quote this guide when booking

A beautiful landscaped garden extending to 75 acres set between two large freshwater lochs. The gardens are famous for their collection of trees and rhododendrons from around the world. The grounds were extensively landscaped in the 18th century, laid out with terraces and avenues. The plant collections include specimens provided by Joseph Hooker and probably the oldest avenue of Monkey Puzzle trees.

Fact File

Opening Times:	1st April - 30th September, seven days a week, 10am - 5pm.
Admission Rates:	Adults £4.00, Senior Citizen £3.00, Child £1.00
Groups Rates:	Minimum group size: 20
	10% discount on normal admission rates.
Facilities:	Tea Shop, Plant Sales.
Disabled Access:	Limited. Toilet and parking for disabled on site.
Tours/Events:	None
Coach Parking:	Yes
Length of Visit:	1 - 4 hours
Booking Contact:	Castle Kennedy Gardens, Stair Estates, Rephad, Stranraer, Dumfries & Galloway, DG9 8BX
	Telephone: 01776 702024 Fax: 01776 706248
Email:	info@castlekennedygardens.co.uk
Website:	www.castlekennedygardens.co.uk
Location:	Approximately 5 miles east of Stranraer on A75.

Drummond Castle Gardens

There is no clue as to what awaits as one drives up a mile-long avenue, closely lined with beech trees. The castle sits on a rocky outcrop and is everything you would expect of an ancient Scottish fortress. Huge walls, a massive keep and spiralling turrets.

On crossing the castle courtyard the gardens are revealed. Standing at the top of a flight of stairs that lead down into the gardens themselves, it is possible to see the full glory of the gardens. Intricate parterres are lined with low box hedges. They depict family crests, contained within a St Andrew's cross. Gravel paths sit alongside neatly clipped yew hedges.

This is a formal Italianate garden sitting amidst the splendour of Scotland's rolling countryside. It is the perfect way to spend a relaxing afternoon walking amongst the plants, exploring the greenhouses or sitting on a bench, soaking up the atmosphere.

Fact File

Opening Times:	Easter Weekend then daily 1st May - 31st October 1pm - 6pm.
Admission Rates:	Adults £3.50, Senior Citizen £2.50, Child £1.50
Groups Rates:	Minimum group size: 20 plus 10% discount on normal admission rates.
Facilities:	Lavatories. Guide book, postcards, soft drinks.
Disabled Access:	Partial. Toilet and parking for disabled on site.
Tours/Events:	Private morning/early evening visits for groups. Guided tours with horticultural or architectural theme. Option to visit the 15th century Tower.
Coach Parking:	Yes
Length of Visit:	Minimum 1 hour.
Booking Contact:	Joe Buchanan Drummond Castle Gardens, Muthill, Crieff, Perthshire, PH5 2AA Telephone: 01764 681257 Fax: 01764 681550
Email:	thegardens@drummondcastle.sol.co.uk
Website:	www.drummondcastlegardens.co.uk
Location:	2 miles south of Crieff off the A822.

Please quote this guide when booking

Dunvegan Castle   Isle of Skye

Extensive Gardens leading from the front of the Castle one makes their way down to the Water Gardens, which include 2 waterfalls, the formal round garden, large walled garden, the new planted woodland garden and various woodland walks. The gardens are skillfully planted with a rare and interesting selection of plants. Any visit to the Isle of Skye must be deemed incomplete without savouring the wealth of history offered by Dunvegan Castle. The seat of the Clan MacLeod for 800 years, Dunvegan Castle is fortress stronghold in an idyllic loch side setting. The Highland Estate has much to offer, including the MacLeod's Table Restaurant providing light snacks to full meals, boat trips to seal colony, audio-visual theatre and a Clan Exhibition. Also there are a variety of shops offering a large range of gifts and souvenirs, high quality wollens, kilts and Country wear. Altogether, a visit to Dunvegan Castle is a fascinating and memorable experience.

Fact File

Opening Times: 22nd March - 31st October, Monday - Sunday 10am - 5.30pm (last entry at 5pm).
November - March, Monday - Sunday 11am - 4pm (last entry at 3.30pm).

Admission Rates: Castle & Gardens - Adults £6.50, Senior Citizen £5.50, Child £3.50 (5-15yrs)
Gardens only - £4.50, Senior Citizen £2.50, Child £2.50

Groups Rates: Minimum group size: 10, Adults £5.50

Facilities: Visitor Centre, Shop, Tea Room, Kiosk, Plant Sales, Seal Boat Trips.

Disabled Access: Not easy access. Toilet for disabled on site.

Tours/Events: None.

Coach Parking: Yes

Length of Visit: 2 plus hours (1 hour house and 1 hour plus grounds)

Booking Contact: Barbara Maclean
Dunvegan Castle, Dunvegan, Isle of Skye, IV55 8WF
Telephone: 01470 521206 Fax: 01470 521205

Email: info@dunvegancastle.com

Website: www.dunvegancastle.com

Location: From Kyle take A87 to Sligachan on the Isle of Skye, turn left onto the A863, this road without deviation will take you directly to Dunvegan Castle.

Please quote this guide when booking

Torosay Castle, completed in 1858 in the Scottish Baronial style by the eminent architect David Bryce, is one of the finer examples of his work, resulting in a combination of elegance and informality, grandeur and homeliness.

A unique combination of formal terraces and dramatic West Highland scenery makes Torosay a spectacular setting, which, together with a mild climate results in superb specimens of rare, unusual and beautiful plants.

A large collection of Statuary and many niche gardens makes Torosay a joy to explore and provides many peaceful corners in which to relax.

Note: No dogs in Gardens please.

Fact File

Opening Times:	House: 1st April - 31st October, 10.30am - 5pm.
	Gardens: Open all year.
Admission Rates:	Adults £5.00, Senior Citizen £4.00, Child £1.75
Groups Rates:	Minimum group size: 10
	Adults £4.00, Senior Citizen £4.00, Child £1.50
Facilities:	Shop, Plant Sales, Tea Room, Holiday Cottages, Parking on site.
Disabled Access:	Yes to gardens only. Toilet and parking for disabled on site.
Tours/Events:	Tours available to groups by arrangement at a cost of £6 per person.
	Concerts, plays etc advertised seperately.
Coach Parking:	Yes
Length of Visit:	2 hours minimum.
Booking Contact:	Mr James/Carol Casey. Torosay Castle, Craignure, Isle of Mull, PA65 6AY
	Telephone: 01680 812421 Fax: 01680 812470
Email:	torosay@aol.com
Website:	www.torosay.com
Location:	1 1/2 miles from Craignure (ferry terminal) on A849/on foot by forest walk or by narrow gauge railway.

Please quote this guide when booking

Wales

"It is warming indeed to see the avenues that I then planted growing so flourishingly and the whole place maturing in ever increasing beauty."

Clough Williams-Ellis

From Cardiff Bay to the mountains of Snowdonia, Wales is a country of contrasts. This is clearly portrayed by the gardens in this book. Here you will find gardens of yesterday and gardens of tomorrow. From the fifteenth century beginnings of Aberglasney to the twenty-first century steel and glass structures of Middleton, there are inspirational gardens in Wales for us all to enjoy.

Opposite: Glansvern Hall Gardens (page 140)

Aberglasney is one of the Country's most exciting garden restoration projects. The Gardens have wonderful horticultural qualities and a mysterious history. Within the nine acres of garden are six different garden spaces including three walled gardens. At its heart is a unique and fully restored Elizabethan/Jacobean cloister garden and a parapet walk, which is the only example that survives in the UK. The Garden already contains a magnificent collection of rare and unusual plants which are seldom seen elsewhere in the country.

The House and Garden will continually be improved over the years, the result will be a world renowned Garden set in the beautiful landscape of the Tywi Valley. There is a Café in the grounds, which serves delectable light lunches and snacks. In the summer, tea can be taken on the terrace overlooking the Pool Garden. There is also a new shop and plant sales area, which can be visited without admission to the garden.

Fact File

Opening Times:	Summer: 10am - 6pm (last entry at 5pm). Winter: 10.30am - 4pm.
Admission Rates:	Adults £5.50, Senior Citizen £4.50, Child £2.50
Groups Rates:	Minimum group size: 10 Adults £5.00, Senior Citizen £4.00, Child £2.50
Facilities:	Shop, Plant Sales, Café.
Disabled Access:	Yes. Toilet and parking for disabled on site. Wheelchairs on loan, booking necessary.
Tours/Events:	Guided tours at 11.30am and 2.30pm.
Coach Parking:	Yes
Length of Visit:	2 - 4 hours
Booking Contact:	Bookings Department Aberglasney Gardens, Llangathen, Carmarthenshire, SA32 8QH Telephone: 01558 668998 Fax: 01558 668998
Email:	info@aberglasney.org.uk
Website:	www.aberglasney.org
Location:	Four miles outside Llandeilo off the A40.

Please quote this guide when booking

Set in the heart of the Vale of Glamorgan countryside, this exceptional example of Edwardian garden design is currently being restored with assistance from the Heritage Lottery Fund. Designed by Thomas Mawson for the avid plant collector Reginald Cory, this unique collaboration has resulted in splendid Great Lawns, intimate garden rooms and an arboretum of rare and unusual trees from around the world. Throughout the restoration the gardens remain open to the public with only sections of the 55 acres of designed landscape closed during the works. Restoration completed in recent years include the Pompeiian Garden, Herbaceous Border, Panel Garden, Reflecting Pool, Heather Garden and Fernery. Ongoing works are focusing on improving access for all visitors and the glasshouse and Walled Kitchen Garden. Enjoy a relaxing stroll or come and see one of the many events taking place throughout the summer.

Fact File

Opening Times: April (or Easter) to September 10am - 6pm, October 10am - 5pm, November - March 10am - 4pm, 7 days a week.

Admission Rates: Adults £3.50, Family (2 Adults & 2 Conc.) £7.00, Conc. £2.50, Disabled £2.00, Carers Free.

Groups Rates: Minimum group size: 15 - Adults £2.50

Facilities: Visitor Centre, Shop, Tea Room, Plant Sales

Disabled Access: Yes. Toilet and parking for disabled on site. Wheelchairs on loan, booking preferable.

Tours/Events: Tours monthly with Head Gardener no additional charge, by arrangement - Charge £1 PP. Varied programme of events from Easter to October.

Coach Parking: Yes   **Length of Visit:** 2 - 3 hours

Booking Contact: Mrs Deborah Kerslake / Mrs Sarah Balmont
Dyffryn Gardens, St Nicholas, Vale of Glamorgan, CF5 6SU
Telephone: 029 20593328   Fax: 029 20591966

Email: slbalmont@valeofglamorgan.gov.uk

Website: www.dyffryngardens.org.uk

Location: Exit M4 at J33 to A4232 (signposted Barry). At roundabout take 1st exit (A4232). At junction with A48/A4050 exit the A4232 at Culverhouse Cross - take 4th exit A48 (signposted Owbirdge). Turn left at lights in St Nicholas Village. Dyffryn on right one and a half miles.

Please quote this guide when booking

Glansevern Hall was built, in Greek Revival style, by Sir Arthur Davies Owen at the turn of the 18th/19th Century.

It looks down on the River Severn from an enclosure of gardens set in wider parkland. Near the house are fine lawns studded with herbaceous and rose beds and a wide border backed by brick walls. A Victorian orangery and a large fountain face each other across the lawns. The large walled garden has been ingeniously divided into compartments separated by hornbeam hedges and ornamental ironwork. There is a rock garden of exceptional size, built of limestone and tufa, which creates a walk-through grotto. A little further afield, woodland walks are laid out around the 4 acre lake and pass through a water garden which, especially in May and June, presents a riot of growth and colour.

Glansevern is noted for its collection of unusual trees.

Fact File

Opening Times:	May - September. Friday, Saturday & Bank Holiday Mondays, 12 noon - 6pm. Group on any other day, booking necessary.
Admission Rates:	Adults £3.50, Senior Citizen £3.00, Child Free
Facilities:	Shop, Tea Room & Light Lunches, Plant Sales, Art Gallery.
Disabled Access:	Yes. Toilet and parking for disabled on site.
Tours/Events:	Guided walk identifying the large number of unusual trees.
Coach Parking:	Yes
Length of Visit:	1 1/2 hours
Booking Contact:	Neville Thomas Glansevern Hall Gardens, Berriew, Welshpool, Powys, SY21 8AH Telephone: 01686 640200 Fax: 01686 640829
Email:	glansevern@onlineuk.co
Website:	www.glansevern.co.uk
Location:	Signposted at Berriew on A483 between Welshpool and Newtown, North Powys.

Middleton, the National Botanic Garden of Wales Carmarthenshire

Set in the glorious parkland of the former regency estate of Middleton Hall, this remarkable 21st century botanic garden is just 7 miles from the market town of Carmarthen.

The spectacular Great Glasshouse embodies the achievements of contemporary architecture and science, whilst the recently restored Double Walled Garden represents horticultural methods of a bygone age combined with an entirely modern approach to planting. A 220m herbaceous Broadwalk, with a small rill running down its length, forming the spine of the garden and leading to the exciting willow play area.

Enjoy a trip on the land train around the lakes and a wander in the Shop amongst the unique branded merchandise, followed by a meal in the Seasons Restaurant.

Fact File

Opening Times: Easter to October 10am - 6pm. British Winter Time to British Summer Time 10am - 4.30pm. Closed Christmas Day.

Admission Rates: Adults £6.95, Senior Citizen £5.00, Child £3.50

Groups Rates: Minimum group size: 10
Adults £5.75, Senior Citizen £4.00, Child £2.50

Facilities: Visitor Centre, Shop, Restaurant, Café, Plant Sales, 360 degree Surround Sound Theatre, Hourly Land Train Tours.

Disabled Access: Yes. Toilet and parking for disabled on site. Wheelchairs on loan, booking necessary.

Tours/Events: Guided tours on request, estate tours weekly and land train tours daily.
Full events programme throughout the year, contact the Garden for events leaflet.

Coach Parking: Yes   **Length of Visit:** 4 hours

Booking Contact: Middleton, the National Botanic Garden of Wales, Llanarthne, Carmarthenshire, SA32 8HG
Telephone: 01558 668768   Fax: 01558 668933

Email: info@gardenofwales.org.uk

Website: www.gardenofwales.org.uk

Location: 10 minutes from the M4 and 1/4 of a mile from the A48 in Carmarthenshire, south west Wales, midway between Cross Hands and Carmarthen.

Please quote this guide when booking

Index

Loseley Park (page 92)

GARDENS TO VISIT 2004 is specially published for:

Publicity Works
P.O. Box 32
Tetbury
Gloucestershire
GL8 8BF
Telephone: 01453 836730   Fax: 01453 835285
Email: mail@publicity-works.org

Press and Media Specialists, Promotion, Publicity and Public Relations Consultants
and Event Organisers.

Thanks go to the Gardens and Garden Visitors who have provided feedback
and the information they would like to see within this publication.

ISBN 1 899803 21 1

Designed, Published and Distributed by:

The WoodLand and Garden Publishing Company
Homeleigh Farm
Huntsgate
Gedney Broadgate
Spalding
Lincs PE12 ODJ

email: derekharris.associates@virgin.net